Cookbook For Begi

YOUR COOKING JOURNEY BEINGS HERE

Fun and Simple Recipes for Beginners To Dip Your Toes in Cooking!

Lina Potts

Table of Contents

PART 1 6

Chapter 1: What Clean Eating Is...7

Chapter 2: Benefits of Clean Eating...10

PART II..12

Chapter 1: How It Works 12

Chapter 2: All About Food 17

Chapter 3: Ketogenic Breakfasts..32

Chapter 4: Ketogenic Lunches 42

Chapter 5: Ketogenic Dinners..53

Chapter 1: The Paleo Diet Benefits You 64

Chapter 1: The Power of the Crock Pot and Its Benefits.......................97

Chapter 2: Healthy Breakfast Recipes..99

Boiled Eggs 99

One-Hour Bread..99

PART V...128

Chapter 3: Soups, Of Course!...138

Chapter 5: Tender Chicken 153

Everyone knows that chicken is the most versatile meat, but combine with a versatile appliance and you have never ending, time efficient and delicious meals!..................153

CHICKEN IN A POT...153

7-9 hours in a slow cooker...153

Yields about 6 servings..153

2 celery ribs, chopped..153

2 medium onions, diced...153

½ teaspoon(s) pepper...153

3 medium carrots, sliced 153

1 ½ teaspoon(s) salt 153

3 medium carrots, sliced 153

1 teaspoon(s) basil..153

3 lbs. chicken..153

½ cup(s) of chicken broth..153

Layer the bottom of the cooker with the vegetables and top with the chicken parts. Mix the final components in a separate bowl and drizzle on top. Cook for 7-9 hours on low. 153

GOLDEN CHICKEN AND NOODLES..154

7-8 hours in the slow cooker...154

Yields about 6 servings..154

1/8 teaspoon(s) pepper 154

1 small chopped onion 154

2-10 ¾ ounce cans of broccoli cheese soup..154

1 teaspoon(s) basil..154

6 chicken breast cut in half 154

2 cup(s) of milk.. 154

1 teaspoon(s) salt 154

Cooked noodles.. 154

Mix together the first 6 ingredients. Place chicken parts in the cooker and top with the mixture. For 7-8 hours, cook on the low setting, until chicken juices run clear. Serve over noodles.. 154

Chapter 6: Flavorful Pork 163

PART 1

Chapter 1: What Clean Eating Is

So, you want to get healthy, feel better, maybe lose a few pounds, and you keep hearing about clean eating everywhere, right? Although at a glance, making the decision to clear your kitchen and eat clean may seem daunting, it doesn't have to be! I promise, clean eating is NOT. THAT. HARD. Before we look at what clean eating really means, let's discuss what it isn't. Clean eating is not:

- A diet. This is not a diet, or a quick fix to shed a few pounds.

- A torture mechanism. You are in no way going to be deprived of the food you love.

- A perfect practice. Clean eating is a journey, not a destination. Clean eating isn't an elitist gimmick or fad, it is a lifestyle change.

Now that you can breathe a little easier knowing that nobody is going to judge you, and that clean eating is not reserved for the perfect and always polished, let's talk about what clean eating really is.

Clean eating is about eliminating foods from your diet that aren't really foods at all, getting rid of foods and ingredients that have zero nutritional benefits, and getting back to basics. Food should feed our bodies, minds, and souls. Food should not be made in a laboratory, genetically toyed with, or leave our bodies unsatisfied and unhealthy. Food is fuel, but it should be fuel we share with our loved ones, enjoyed, and above all, good for us!

Let's Get Started

Where does one begin the journey to kicking the junk? Well, that really depends on how far you are willing to take things, and your comfort level. Everyone wants to look and feel better, and clean eating will help you achieve those goals. But, almost everything in your pantry and kitchen is full of stuff you do not need. Below is an idea of where to start cleaning up your diet for the better.

Kick the preservatives, chemicals, and processed food.

I know this seems daunting when you really consider what is on the grocery store shelves today, but you can start small. Chips are great and all, but check out that back label. Can you pronounce all the ingredients and do you know what they are? Are there more than 5 ingredients? Can you thinly slice potatoes and bake or broil them? If you answered no to all the above questions, you may starve. Just kidding! The point here is to really think about what is in those chips, and whether you are ready to either substitute them in your diet, or if it is easier to eliminate them all together. You can eat what you want, but do you really think those bagged chips are fueling your body in a healthy way considering the label?

Eliminate GMO foods wherever you can

And while chips are an easy target, consider the ears of corn at your local grocers. They are big, bright, and look really yummy, but so very bad. Most corn is genetically modified, so check the stickers, take note of the display, or ask an employee. Buying certified organic fresh produce is a great way to ensure that your food is GMO free. Organic does sometimes cost more, but buying seasonal produce from a local market is usually not any costlier than what you can get at major chain grocery stores. And, you are doing your local economy a huge favor. To start small, consider buying organic, and replacing your current selections of the notorious top ten listed below.

The top 10 genetically modified foods are:

- Soy
- Dairy Products
- Corn
- Rice
- Tomatoes
- Potatoes
- Canola
- Papaya
- Peas

The list above is a good place to start. The goal is to get clean, not stress yourself out. There is no shame in starting small and working your way from there. Any positive, healthy changes will have your body thanking you, Trust me.

Chapter 2: Benefits of Clean Eating

So, what are the benefits of eating clean? Consider that you are getting rid of foods that are not only lacking nutritional value, but that these foods also contain a varying array of toxins, poisons, and additives that can make you prone to illnesses that can literally kill you. Clean eating will eliminate the garbage, and fill your body with nutrient rich foods. Foods that are dense in nutrients help your body build and maintain a healthier gut, which in turn translates into a healthier, more effective immune system. You will not only be less likely to get sick, you will also be decreasing your chances of forming chronic illnesses, many of which are linked to the chemicals, preservatives, and GMO's that many people ingest daily.

Another awesome side effect of eating clean is that by eating cleaner, you are eating healthier. Most people that make the change report healthy, steady, weight loss, and that is a bonus for most of us! Eating clean foods chock full of nutrition, you will also feel fuller on less weight per average meal. Imagine a wrap that weighs 6 ounces filling you up better than a frozen pizza that weighs 16 ounces, and gives you more energy. Speaking of energy...

Eating clean will give you more energy, and your energy levels will maintain better throughout the course of the day. By eliminating empty carbohydrates, refined and sugar foods, and steering clear of refined grains, your body will begin regulate its insulin levels naturally. No spike in blood sugar equals no sugar crash later.

Clean eating also encourages an increase in Omega-3 fatty acids in your diet, which help your brain. B complex vitamins are good for your entire system, and increase serotonin and dopamine chemicals released by the brain, making you feel happier. And, Omega-3 fatty acids have been shown to reduce moodiness and even help decrease depression. Another benefit to eating clean is that you will sleep better too! Passing on a cookie and milk before bed and instead noshing on a handful of almonds (which contain tryptophan) and skim milk (that offers us melatonin) will help you sleep like a baby, and wake up refreshed. There are a thousand reasons why clean eating is good for you, and your body will only thank you!

PART II

Chapter 1: How It Works

There are so many different diet plans out there, it can be confusing and overwhelming

when you are deciding which one would work best for you. Some of these diets are trends or fads and not something that can be maintained long-term, others might make you feel hungry all the time, which as you know, does not make for a happy life. This is one of the reasons the ketogenic diet stands apart from the rest, it will help you lose weight, while also letting you feel satisfied. You are not starving your body of calories or fat on the ketogenic diet.

What Does Ketogenic Mean?

When you eat a more traditional diet that is higher in carbohydrates your body produces glucose and insulin. Glucose is the body's first choice of energy source because it is the easiest for the body to convert. Insulin's role is to process the glucose that is in your bloodstream by taking it around the body. When this happens, it means that the fats in your body are not needed, since they are not the energy source. The fat still has to go somewhere though, so the body stores it for later use.

When you lower your carbohydrate intake, your body will enter into a state known as ketosis, which is where the word ketogenic comes from. Ketosis is what the body initiates when food consumption is low, it is a natural process that is meant to help the body survive. During ketosis the liver will break down fats and produce ketones which can also be used as fuel for the body, but only if glucose is in short supply. Remember, glucose is the body's first choice, so it will only use something else when glucose is not an option. It is not because it can't or that is not healthy, when using ketones as fuel, the body just has to work a little harder.

The goal of the ketogenic diet is to get your body to switch from using glucose as its fuel supply, to ketones, which you would get from the breakdown of fat. Therefore, your body would be getting all its energy from fat. As your insulin levels lower, your body's fat burning abilities will increase. For most people, this happens very quickly and quite dramatically. One of the benefits of this diet is how easy it becomes to burn through stored fat, which obviously helps if weight loss is your main goal.

The quickest way to enter ketosis is by fasting, however that cannot be maintained without harmful effects. The ketogenic diet can be followed indefinitely, while still allowing the body to enter ketosis. This is not a diet that deals with calorie counting, meaning you cannot eat what ever you want as long as you don't go over your caloric limit. Keeping your carbohydrate intake low, it is suggested no more than 20 or 30g of net carbohydrates is how you will be successful. However, the less you consume, the more dramatic your weight loss will be.

What is a Net Carb?

Net carb = Total dietary carbohydrate – Total fiber

Let's assume you want to eat one cup of broccoli, which contains 6g of total carbohydrates and 2g of fiber. To find the net carbs, you would then take the 6g minus the 2g, leaving you with 4g, which is the net carb amount.

Your ketogenic diet should be made of around 70 percent fats, 25 percent proteins, and only 5 percent should be carbohydrates. This is why it is so important to pay attention to what you are putting into your body and whether or not it will prevent you from entering ketosis.

The ketogenic diet will yield impressive results, but only if you stick to it. When you eat too many carbohydrates, your body will have the insulin it needs to use as fuel, meaning the fat will be stored instead of burned. The secret to a successful ketogenic diet is to plan-out what you will eat, this will not only reduce your stress, but it will also keep you on the right track.

Just like any diet or lifestyle change, it will take time for you to properly adjust to it, but you can do it. One of the best things you can do for yourself is to keep an open mind and allow yourself the time necessary to acclimate. Rushing things before you are fully prepared will not help you, it will only cause you added stress which will probably lead to failure. To prevent this from happening, it is crucial that you find what works for you while still adhering to the diet.

Some people prefer to prep their meals a head of time, especially breakfast and lunch since they often take it with them to work. Other people like to write out their meals like a menu and stick with their ideas. You don't have to do this, but it definitely make things easier on you, especially in the beginning.

When you are on a special diet like this one, it probably won't take you very long to see how much easier it is to cook at home. Being in complete control of your food is crucial to remaining in ketosis and losing weight. That being said, if you do decide to go to a restaurant, make sure to ask any appropriate questions involving your order. Being specific about what foods are cooked in or how they are prepared will help make sure you are sticking to your diet.

Just remember, you are not going to be hungry, your body is learning to depend a different fuel for energy. That takes some time to get accustomed to, so be patient with yourself and find what works best for you. For instance, if you prefer to prep all of your meals for the week on Sunday, do it. However, if you work the night shift and enjoy cooking when you arrive home in the morning, feel free to do it that way, just find what works for you and stick to it.

Chapter 2: All About Food

Starting a new diet can be frustrating and irritating, especially if you think you are sticking to the rules, but are not seeing any positive results. This is why it is so important to know exactly what you are allowed to eat what you are not. If you don't know what foods are acceptable and are not knowledgeable about your diet, you won't be successful, regardless of the effort you are putting forth. So, make it easy on yourself and learn which foods you should eat and which you should avoid.

The best way to think of the ketogenic diet is to think real, whole foods. Anything that is prepackaged or processed is full of net carbohydrates and is off limits. This means staying away from pastas, cereals, breads, and cakes. Fruits and vegetables also contain carbohydrates so it is important that you also keep track of these net carbs as well. You already know that your diet is going to consist of mostly healthy fats, but you might understand what that means exactly. Well, first, not all fats are equal, some are definitely better for you than others and it is crucial that you know the difference.

Fats, Good and Bad

Foods contain different types of fats, but are categorized by what they contain the most of. For instance, butter is considered a saturated fat because it contains 60 percent saturated fat. As you move forward with your diet you will quickly understand the role fats play, without them you would be hungry all the time and would be left feeling unsatisfied.

Saturated Fats – These are known as essential to our health as they help to keep our immune systems healthy. In addition to helping with the immune system, this fat will also help balance hormone levels and maintain a normal bone density. This type of fat has a bad reputation and time and again has been included in the 'bad for you' category, but many different studies have shown that they are important and necessary for a healthy body. Meats, butter, and eggs all have saturated fats in them.

Polyunsaturated Fats – This is the type of fat that is commonly found in vegetable oils, and for a long time they were thought to be beneficial. However, that is not the case as they are often over processed, for instance, "heart healthy" margarines have been linked to heart disease. Yet, polyunsaturated fats that are natural such as those found in fish actually help to lower cholesterol, so it is important to know the difference and not get them confused. This is why real, natural foods are so important because the fats they contain are much better for you than their highly processed counterparts.

Monounsaturated Fats – This is an accepted healthy fat, as it improves insulin resistance and cholesterol levels. This type of fat is found in both sunflower and olive oils, both of which are common and easy to incorporate into your diet.

Trans Fats – You probably already know that trans fats are not good for you, they do not occur in natural fatty foods, only processed fatty foods. That is an important distinction, because this type of fat is created from chemicals that are used to extend a food's shelf-life. For instance, the hydrogenation process is when hydrogen is added to these fats which changes their chemical make-up. Even if a label does not say it contains trans fats, if it says hydrogenated on it, avoid it.

When you are doing your grocery shopping, try to purchase organic products and grass-fed proteins. Avoid canned or frozen fruits and vegetables too, but it is understandable that some people just do not have the financial means to do this, so be cautious and make sure you read all the labels. The next chapters are going to contain some recipes that you can try, but as you progress with your diet, you will see how easy it is to incorporate healthy fats into your meals. This will help you feel satisfied and will help you stay fuller longer.

Fats:

Avocado

Beef Tallow

Chicken Fat

Macadamia Nuts

Ghee

Butter

Non-hydrogenated Lard

Mayonnaise – read the label and make sure it does not have added carbs.

Red palm oil

Peanut butter

Olive oil

Coconut oil

Proteins:

Fish – Try to purchase wild caught if available, this can include salmon, trout, catfish, halibut, cod, flounder, mackerel, tuna, and snapper.

Shellfish – Crab, oysters, mussels, squid, lobster, scallops, and clams.

Whole Eggs – Opt for free-range if you can, local organic farmers often have them cheaper than your local grocery stores. When it comes to preparation you have many different options such as boiled, poached, scrambled, deviled, and fried.

Meat – Grass-fed typically has a higher fatty acid count, so opt for grass-fed when given the opportunity. Goat, lamb, veal, beef, and other wild game are all good choices.

Pork – You can eat nearly any type of pork, just make sure to read the label to make sure there are no added sugars.

Poultry – Pheasant, quail, chicken, and duck are all acceptable, but choose free range and organic if it is possible.

Sausage and Bacon – This can still be an acceptable and even beneficial protein as long as you choose it wisely, make sure there are no extra fillers and that it is not cured in sugar.

Peanut Butter – Choose natural peanut butter, but make sure to read the label carefully, even the most natural peanut butter can contain high amounts of carbohydrates, a better alternative is macadamia nut butter.

Vegetables

The best vegetables to eat on the ketogenic diet are those that are leafy and grow above ground. Again, if you can eat organic, try to do so as there will less pesticides used in the growing process, but if you can't try not to worry too much. Studies have shown that both non-organic and organic vegetables have the same nutritional qualities.

Of course vegetables are good for you, but some are better than others in terms of the ketogenic diet. For instance, some vegetables are high in sugar and lower in important nutrients, these are the types of vegetables that you want to either cut out altogether or consume only in very small portions. The best vegetables for this diet are those that are low in carbohydrates and high in nutrients, such as kale and anything green leafy that resembles it. These types of veggies are also easy to include in meals and they really pack a powerful nutrition punch as well.

Remember, vegetables also contain carbohydrates, so make sure you are keeping track throughout the day so you stay well within the acceptable limit. The following is a list of vegetables and their net carbohydrates by ounce.

Avocado - .6

Broccoli – 1.1

Baby Carrots – 1.5

Cauliflower - .5

Celery - .3

Cucumber – 1

Green Beans – 1.3

Mushrooms - .6

Green Onion – 1.3

White Onion – 2.1

Green Pepper - .8

Romaine Lettuce - .3

Butterhead Lettuce - .3

Shallots – 3.9

Snow Peas – 2.8

Spinach - .4

Acorn Squash – 2.9

Butternut Squash – 2.1

Spaghetti Squash – 1.4

Tomato - .8

As you begin making your own meal plans, simply add up the net carbohydrates between the different foods so you have an idea of how many you are consuming from that meal. This will get easier over time, you can even try writing it down in the beginning until you get more comfortable keeping track.

Dairy

Dairy products are also acceptable as long as there is no added sugars or other additives. It is best to go choose full fat, raw, and organic.

Sour Cream

Cottage Cheese

Heavy Whipping Cream

Hard and Soft Cheeses (Cream cheese, cheddar, mozzarella, mascarpone, etc)

You probably are guessed what is going to be said next, but it really can't be stressed enough, make sure you read the labels. Many cheeses are low in net carbohydrates as it is, but if you are in doubt either read the label or as the person behind the counter.

Nuts and Seeds

Seeds and nuts are a great way to add healthy fats to your diet and make a wonderful and convenient snack. It is best to eat them when they are roasted, this process removes any anti-nutrients. It is also important to note that there is a difference between a nut and a legume, nuts are allowed, while legumes are generally not permitted. Oddly enough, based on the name, a peanut is a legume and should be avoided. Here is a list of acceptable nuts and seeds:

Macadamias, walnuts, and almonds, all of these should be eaten in moderation, but their carbohydrate count is relatively low.

Pistachios and cashews are both higher in carbohydrates, but do contain healthy fats, so make sure you keep careful track of them.

Tip: Seed and nut flower are good alternatives to white or wheat flour, but try not to make this a staple in your diet because nuts are high in Omega-6 fatty acids, so be careful with over eating them because it can lead to weight gain and slow your progress.

Beverages

When you start your ketogenic diet, you will notice that it will have a natural diuretic effect, which means hydration is even more important. Also, if you are someone who is prone to bladder pain or urinary tract infections, you will need to be even more diligent when it comes to hydrating. It is suggested that you not only drink the recommended eight glasses of water each day, more in addition. Our bodies are made up of 2/3 water, so make sure you are keeping it happy and hydrated. Drink appropriate liquids like it is going out of style!

Water, drink it. Drink a lot of it.

Coffee, with heavy cream and no sugar, it is fine in moderation.

Tea, also no added sugar and if you like it with milk make sure it is raw and whole fat or use heavy cream.

Sweeteners

Of course it is best to avoid anything that is sweet, but for some of us with a sweet tooth, this would just make us miserable. That being said, if you have a sweet craving that you can't seem to deny, choose an artificial sweetener and try not to do this often. Liquid sweeteners are better since there are no added binders like in the powder forms that have carbohydrates.

Stevia

Sucralose

Monk Fruit

Erythirol

Xylitol

Spices

When it comes to what you eat, you want it to be flavorful and satisfying, most of which will come from the addition of spices. However, many spices contain carbohydrates, so it is important that you keep track of the amounts of you are using and add those amounts to your carbohydrate total for your meal. You can use nearly any dry spices you prefer, just make sure you look up the carbohydrate content, no one wants your food to be boring and bland. Some spices have more carbs than others, such as cinnamon, garlic powder, allspice, bay leaves, ginger, and cardamom, so if those are staples in your cooking, make sure you are keeping accurate track.

Watch Out For

Fruit – Limit your fruit content because fruit is high in natural sugars and therefore carbohydrates. Many people use berries in desserts or as snacks, but only in small portions and not very often. If you choose to do this, be cautious of raspberries, cranberries, and blueberries.

Tomato – Food companies are very good at making their products look healthier than they really are. Tomatoes do have natural sugars in them, but when you buy tomato based products additional sugar is often added. That doesn't mean you can't use canned tomato sauces or diced tomatoes, just make sure you read the labels.

Peppers – Most of us do not think of peppers as being full of sugars, green has the last amount of sugars compared to red or yellow.

Diet Sodas – You can still drink diet soda, just pay close attention to how much you are drinking and try to limit yourself if you are soda dependent. Some people have reported that they were knocked out of ketosis from consuming too much artificial sweetener, so just keep that in mind when you are considering a diet soda.

Salt – Since the ketogenic diet acts as a natural diuretic, you will see that your body does not retain salt the same way it did before. This means that salt and other electrolytes are flushed from the body very quickly, this can lead to many different health issues such as panic attacks and heart palpitations. To prevent this from happening you can include salted bone broth into your diet or you can use what is known as a light salt that is a combination of both salt and potassium. Most people also choose to take a supplement for anything they think are not getting enough of from their diet.

Water – When you think you have consumed enough water, drink a little more. Your body is going through some huge changes and part of that is flushing out liquids faster than before, so to keep yourself healthy it is a good idea to drink water, a lot of water.

In The Beginning

If this your first time embarking on a low carbohydrate diet, there are some things you need to know. Your body is doing to go through what is known as detox symptoms, this is perfectly natural, but uncomfortable. Remember, you are retraining your body, that doesn't happen without consequences. However, don't be discouraged, they only last for a few days and no matter how bad it feels, you can and will get through it.

These withdrawal symptoms are commonly referred to as the "keto flu," which sounds much worse than it is. Just keep telling yourself that the first three days are the hardest and it will get much easier after. Here is a list of the symptoms:

Irritability

Fatigue

Dizziness

Intense Cravings

Basically, your body is acting like an unruly child who wants sugar, because it has become so accustomed to it. For those who are transitioning from a very carbohydrate dense diet the symptoms will be much worse than others, it just depends on the person's body. Just don't give up. There are some things you can do to help cope with the negative side effects by increasing your water intake. When the very intense cravings hit, and they will, give your body something to eat, just not what it wants, try bacon or cheese. You are not denying yourself food, just distracting it from craving carbohydrates, until you adjust, distraction is the key to success.

Benefits

Now that you just read about the negative side effects, you might be feeling even more overwhelmed than before. However, the benefits of the ketogenic diet far outweighs the negative. Here is a list of the benefits:

Less appetite – After your body has had time to adjust to ketosis, your appetite will just naturally be reduced. This will also eventually lead to less calorie intake too.

Weight Loss – Not only will you lose weight on this diet, but not all fat is the same. When you hold more fat in the abdominal area, this can cause many different health issues, even increasing your risk of heart disease. The ketogenic diet will help you lose weight in the abdominal area, and usually rather quickly, this will help those who are risk for type 2 diabetes as well as heart disease.

Blood Pressure – The ketogenic diet helps to reduce high blood pressure and is often suggested by doctors for this reason.

The Brain – Some parts of the brain can only use glucose which is why our liver will create glucose from protein when we do not eat carbohydrates. However, most of the brain is capable of using ketones as fuel. Allowing the brain to use ketones as fuel has helped many children and adults alike with epilepsy. Currently, scientists are looking into a connection between the ketogenic diet and Alzheimer's disease.

Now, you have an idea of what you are going to be eating and how to count the net carbohydrates in the foods. When you first start out, keep very close track of your portion sizes so you can keep an accurate record of the net carbs. If you are choosing to remain under 20 net carbohydrates a day, then make sure to include not only the ingredients from the meal you are eating, but also from the beverage and even the spices. You will want to do this for each meal so you know for sure you are not exceeding your limit.

This is probably not going to come very easily in the beginning, but rest assured, it will get easier for you. Also, after you stick to the diet for a couple of weeks, you will already start to see results and nothing works to motivate quite like seeing the desired results. Even if it feels like you just can't keep going, or you want to give up, don't, it was hard for nearly everyone in the beginning. You are going through something huge, retraining your brain and learning to control your cravings. Chances are, you are also breaking some bad habits as well, so give yourself the necessary time to fully adjust.

Chapter 3: Ketogenic Breakfasts

This is a collection of ketogenic recipes that you can mix and match to give you a three week jump start on your diet. This will help you by taking the guess work out of what to make and it will also give you a general idea of how to prepare the correct foods for yourself. Once you start your new diet, you might find that you choose to meal prep for the week, and if that is the case, make sure your choices are able to be stored appropriately.

Many people think breakfast is one of the hardest meals to create because you can only eat so many eggs and bacon before you are craving variety. For that purpose, traditional eggs and bacon or sausage are going to be avoided, in favor of other easy and more creative options.

Egg Porridge

1/3 cup heavy cream

2 eggs

Cinnamon to taste

2 tablespoons butter

Berries, optional

Sweetener, optional

This is a ketogenic version of oatmeal or porridge, it is based on how eggs curdle and uses that grainy feel as added texture. You can choose whether or not to add berries or sweetener, depending on how many carbohydrates you are allotting yourself.

1. Combine the cream, eggs, and sweetener if you choose to use it in a small bowl and whisk the mixture together until uniform in color.

2. In a saucepan melt the butter over medium-high heat, but keep an eye on it and do not allow it to turn brown. Once the butter is melted, turn the heat to low.

3. Add the cream and egg mixture to the butter in the saucepan, make sure you continue mixing, especially along the bottom because that is where it will start to curdle and thicken first. Once you start to see the little grains or curdles remove it from the heat.

4. Add a serving to a bowl and sprinkle the top with cinnamon and the berries if you choose.

Cream Cheese Pancakes

2 eggs

½ teaspoon cinnamon

2 ounces of cream cheese (read the label and make sure there are no added sugars)

1 teaspoon sweetener, optional

Butter, to grease pan

You will also need a blender or a food processor for this recipe.

1. Place all the ingredients into the blender or food processor and mix until smooth. Sit it aside and allow it to rest for two or three minutes, or until the bubbles are settled.

2. Grease the pan and set it on medium high heat, with the butter and pour the batter onto the pan, just like you would with traditional pancakes. Cook for two minutes and then flip, cook for an additional minute or until golden brown. Repeat this until all of the batter has been used.

3. You can eat these with sugar-free syrup, berries, or nothing at all depending on what your carbohydrate limit is.

This is a great recipe to make for large groups since it is so easy and quick. They will make a great addition to your diet and will leave you feeling full and satisfied.

Lemon Poppy Seed Muffins

2 tablespoons poppy seeds

Zest of 2 lemons

3 tablespoons lemon juice

3 large eggs

¾ cup almond flour

¼ cup flaxseed meal

1 teaspoon vanilla extract

¼ cup heavy cream

1/3 cup erythritol

1 teaspoon baking powder

¼ salted butter, melted

25 drops of liquid sweetener

Muffin pan and liners

1. Set your oven to 250F, and in a bowl combine the flaxseed meal, poppy seeds, almond flour, and erythritol.

2. Slowly pour in the eggs and heavy cream, stir constantly until the mixture is smooth and there are no lumps in the batter.

3. Once the mixture is smooth add the sweetener, vanilla extract, lemon juice, lemon zest, and baking powder. Make sure to stir this well to ensure everything is mixed together properly.

4. Put your liners in the muffin pan, or silicone molds, this batter will make 12 muffins, but if you need to you can adjust the size a little, just try not to make them too big.

5. Place your batter in the oven and bake for 18 to 20 minutes, if you want a crispier crust on the bottom, leave them in for a bit longer.

6. When they are finished baking, take them out of the oven and let them rest on the counter for around 10 minutes.

These are the perfect breakfast for people who want something they can easily take with them. If you know you are in for a busy week, these make for a great breakfast to make before your work week starts.

'McGriddle' Casserole

10 eggs

1 cup almond flour

¼ cup flaxseed meal

1 pound breakfast sausage

½ teaspoon onion powder

½ teaspoon garlic powder

¼ teaspoon sage

4 tablespoons sage

4 ounce cheddar cheese

6 tablespoons sugar free syrup

Salt and pepper to taste

Casserole pan

Parchment paper

1. Preheat the oven to 350F and put a pan on medium heat, this is for the breakfast sausage. You are going to break it up as you brown it.
2. In a large mixing bowl combine all of the dry ingredients, mix them together and then add the wet ingredients, but only put in 4 tablespoons of the syrup. Mix everything together until is uniform and smooth.

3.   After your mixture is mixed well, add the cheese and stir some more.

4.   Throughout this process, you should also be checking on your sausage to make sure it is not getting too brown, you just want it to be a little crispy. When it is cooked to your liking, pour it, with the fat, into the mixture and stir everything together.

5.   Place the parchment paper into your casserole pan and pour the mixture into the dish. Drizzle the remaining syrup over the top of the mixture.

6.   Bake for about 45 to 55 minutes, if your pan is larger and your casserole thinner, you will need to adjust the cooking time to a bit less. You want the inside to be cooked through completely though, you'll know it is when it is golden brown and looks firm.

7.   When it is done cooking, remove it from the oven and gently pull out the parchment paper, slice the casserole into pieces and serve with either sugar-free ketchup, or even a little more syrup.

This is a great recipe that you can eat all week. Feel free to alter the recipe to suit your needs, for instance, if you think it is too much syrup, you can adjust the amount.

Breakfast Tacos

6 eggs

3 strips of bacon

½ avocado

1 cup shredded mozzarella, make sure it is whole milk

1 ounce shredded cheddar cheese

2 tablespoons butter

Salt and pepper to taste

1. First, you are going to cook the bacon, the easiest way is to preheat your oven to 375F and bake it for 15 to 20 minutes, but if you choose to cook it in a pan, that's fine too.

2. While the bacon is cooking, put 1/3 of a cup of mozzarella in a clean pan on medium heat. You want it to be uniform in thickness and in a circle, this is what will be your taco shell. Be patient, this takes some practice to get right, but you'll get the hang of it.

3. After about two or three minutes the edges will be brown, this is when you are going to carefully slide a spatula underneath it. If you used whole milk mozzarella this should be easy since the oils in it prevent it from sticking naturally.

4. Rest a wooden spoon over a large bowl, using either tongs or your spatula, gently drape the mozzarella over the spoon so as it hardens it will be in the shape of a crunchy taco shell. Do this to the rest of the mozzarella, which will leave you with three completed shells when finished.

5. Your next step is to cook your eggs in the butter, you can do a soft or a hard scramble, it's your preference.

6. When your eggs are finished, spoon them into each of your taco shells and add the sliced avocado on top. Then top with our bacon, you can simply place the entire slice on each, or dice it up.

7. The final step is to sprinkle the cheddar cheese on each taco and enjoy.

This is a breakfast that helps people transition when they are craving that crunch that carbohydrates provides. So, if you find yourself craving chips or breads, this might help satisfy you. Keep in mind though, that even though these do not take too long to make, they are not like the casserole where you can make extra for the week. You are pretty much just making a serving at a time.

Brownie Muffins

¼ cup cocoa powder

1 cup flaxseed meal

½ tablespoon baking powder

1 egg

1 tablespoon cinnamon

2 tablespoons coconut oil

½ teaspoon salt

½ pumpkin puree, if canned read the label carefully

¼ sugar-free caramel syrup

1 teaspoon apple cider vinegar

¼ slivered almonds

1 teaspoon vanilla extract

1. Preheat your oven to 350F and put all the dry ingredients into a large mixing bowl.

2. In a separate mixing bowl combine all the wet ingredients and stir until uniform and smooth.

3. Gently pour the wet ingredients into the dry bowl and mix together until everything is smooth and it is smooth.

4. Put your muffin liners into your pan and spoon about ¼ cup of batter into each one, and sprinkle the almonds over the top, press them down slightly so they don't fall off. This recipe will make 6 muffins, if you need 12, simply double all of the ingredients.

5. Place them in the oven and check on them after about 15 minutes, you will know they're done when they rise. You can eat them either cold or warm, they make the perfect addition to your morning coffee.

This is the perfect breakfast for anyone who has a sweet tooth. So, for those who are starting a low carbohydrate diet for the first time, these can help with those intense sweet carb cravings. You should not feel hungry and unsatisfied on your diet and this is a great way to make sure that doesn't happen.

These breakfasts can be mixed and matched throughout the weeks, or you can make the casserole and eat it for the whole week. You can even freeze individual servings and microwave it when needed. You want your diet to work around your life, not change your life to work around your diet. Too many huge changes at one time can lead to failure. So, find what meals work for you and stick to it, for instance, if you are more likely to hit the snooze button on your alarm and find yourself rushing, setting aside time to cook an elaborate breakfast, might not be feasible. If that is the case, the casserole or the muffins would be best for you.

Chapter 4: Ketogenic Lunches

When it comes to ketogenic friendly foods, it is usually best if you prepare them at home so you know exactly what you're eating. If you have a tendency to go out to lunch when you are at work, bringing it might seem strange in the beginning. However, it is easier than trying to find ketogenic friendly foods on a menu that does not usually have them specifically listed. Going out to eat can be frustrating because you will need to ask the server so many different questions about ingredients. Until you are more comfortable and confident with your diet, it is a good idea to bring your lunch with you, just to ensure that you remain in ketosis.

Just like with the breakfasts, you can make your lunches daily if you choose, or you can prep things a head of time. Some people prefer to only make lunches that can frozen in individual servings so all they have to do is thrown the Tupperware into their lunchbox and be on their way. Others prefer to prepare their lunch night before or their morning of work, depending on time and what they are in the mood for. The following recipes are all easy and quick, and fit well with the mix and match three week plan.

Mixed Green Salad

3 tablespoons roasted pine nuts

2 tablespoons shaved parmesan

2 ounces of mixed greens

2 slices of bacon

Salt and pepper to taste

Ketogenic friendly dressing of your choice, read the label carefully

1. Cook the bacon until it is crispy, you can do this the oven or in a pan, it is up to you. Some people prefer to burn the edges just a bit to add bitter notes to the salad, this complements vinaigrette dressings especially well.
2. Put your portioned greens into a container that has a lid with some extra room, this is for shaking purposes, so keep that in mind when choosing.
3. Crumble the bacon into the greens and toss in the rest of the ingredients including the dressing. Put the lid on the top and shake the container until the dressing coats the greens evenly.

If you are taking this with you to work, wait until you get to work to combine the ingredients. You can keep them separate in reusable bags or in small containers. This helps to keep the salad from getting soggy.

Pigs in a Keto Blanket

37 small sausages, read the label carefully

1 egg

1.5 ounces of cream cheese

8 ounces of cheddar cheese

¾ almond flour

1 tablespoon psyllium husk powder, or coconut flour

Salt and pepper to taste

1. Combine all the dry ingredients in a large bowl.

2. Melt the cheddar cheese in 20 second intervals in the microwave, stir carefully to ensure it is melting evenly. It is done when it is completely melted and slightly bubbling on the outside.

3. Mix together all the ingredients while the cheddar is still hot, this will be your dough.

4. Spread the dough out in a flat and even sheet, make sure it is not too thick, you have 37 sausages to cover after all.

5. Preheat your oven to 400F and put the dough in the refrigerator for 15 to 20 minutes to let it harden up a bit.

6. Once it is cold, slice the dough into strips, a pizza cutter is perfect for this, and wrap them around the sausages. Put them in the oven and bake them for 13 to 15 minutes, before you remove them, broil them for an additional one or two minutes.

These make a great lunch because they can be reheated once you get to work. You can eat them with a sugar-free ketchup or mustard if you choose. In addition to making a convenient lunch, these also make the perfect snack to bring to a party. When you go to gatherings or parties you might find that there is a lack of ketogenic snacks. Unless otherwise specified, it is safe to assume that you might be faced with a table full of foods you can't eat. The easy solution is to bring your own, these are perfect for that.

Tuna Melt Balls with Avocado

10 ounce canned tuna, drained

1 avocado

1/3 cup almond flour

¼ cup mayonnaise, read the label to check for added sugars

¼ cup parmesan cheese

¼ teaspoon onion powder

½ teaspoon garlic powder

Salt and pepper to taste

½ coconut oil for frying, approximately a ¼ cup will be absorbed

1. Drain the tuna and put it a bowl that is large enough to hold all of the ingredients.
2. Add the parmesan cheese, spices, and mayonnaise to the tuna and mix it together until evenly coated.
3. Slice your avocado in half and carefully take out the pit, cube the inside. If you have a way that you prefer to cut avocados, feel free to do what makes you comfortable, just make sure the pieces are in small cubes.
4. Add the avocado in with the rest of the mixture, but fold it in slowly, try not to mash it too much, you want pieces to remain.

5. Roll the mixture into balls, about the size of traditional meat balls. Then roll them in the almond flour, make sure they are evenly coated.

6. Put the coconut oil in a pan on medium heat, when it is hot add the tuna balls and fry them until they are brown and crisp on the outside. Make sure you are turning them to ensure each side is cooked properly.

7. Now, simply remove from the pan and serve.

These are a great ketogenic version of a tuna melt, you get the creamy center and the added crunch of the outside. Granted, they are not going to be as crunchy when they are reheated, but they are still delicious and easy to take to work with you.

Pizza Frittata

9 ounce bag frozen spinach

12 eggs

1 ounce pepperoni

1 teaspoon minced garlic

5 ounce mozzarella cheese

½ cup parmesan cheese

½ cup fresh ricotta cheese

4 tablespoons olive oil

¼ teaspoon nutmeg

Salt and pepper to taste

Iron skillet or glass container

1. Microwave the frozen spinach for three to four minutes, you don't want to be hot, just defrosted. Then squeeze the spinach with your hands to remove as much water as you can and then set it aside.

2. Preheat your oven to 375F and while it is getting hot, mix together the olive oil, eggs, and spices. Stir or whisk this together until everything is combined.

3. Break the spinach up into small pieces and toss it in the mixture. Next, add the parmesan and ricotta cheeses and mix everything together until it is well combined.

4. Pour your mixture into the skillet and then cover with the mozzarella, place the pepperoni on top just like you would a traditional pizza.

5. Put in the oven and bake for 30 minutes if you are using the cast iron skillet, add an additional 10 to 15 minutes if it is glass. You might need to adjust the baking time depending on the thickness of the frittata, but you will know when it is done when it is slightly browned and firm.

6. Then, just slice and serve.

This a perfect lunch to make at the beginning of the week, that will provide enough servings to last the entire week. It is easy to bring to work and once you are there, you can simply heat it up.

Chicken and BBQ Soup

Base

2 teaspoons chili seasoning

3 chicken thighs

1 ½ cups chicken broth

2 tablespoons of olive oil or chicken fat

1 ½ cups of beef broth

Salt and pepper to taste

Sauce

1 tablespoon hot sauce

¼ cup reduced sugar ketchup

2 tablespoons Dijon mustard

¼ cup tomato paste

1 teaspoon Worcestershire sauce

2 1.2 teaspoon liquid smoke

1 tablespoon soy sauce

1 teaspoon onion powder

1 teaspoon red chili flakes

1 teaspoon chili powder

1 teaspoon cumin

¼ cup butter

1 ½ teaspoons garlic powder

Crock pot or slow cooker

1. Preheat the oven to 400F and remove the bones from the chicken thighs and keep the bones. Season the chicken with some of the chili seasoning and put on a baking tray that is lined with foil.

2. Place the chicken in the oven and bake for 50 minutes.

3. While the chicken is in the oven, grab a pot and add the chicken fat or olive oil, heat this on medium high heat and when it is hot put the chicken bones into the oil and cook them for five minutes. Next, add the broth and season with salt and pepper to taste.

4. When the chicken is done baking, take them out and remove the skins and set aside. Pour the fat from the baked chicken into the broth, stirring occasionally.

5. Now you are going to BBQ sauce by combining all of the ingredients listed above. Then add it to the large pot and stir everything together. Let the mixture simmer for about 20 to 30 minutes.

6. After it has had time to simmer, use an immersion blender, this will emulsify the liquids and fats together. Shred the chicken and put it in the soup, you can also add bell pepper or spring onions during this step if you choose to and simmer for another 10 to 20 minutes.

7. After it has had time to thicken up, you can now serve it up. You can garnish it with a little cheddar cheese, onions, or some diced up green peppers. The crispy chicken you set aside should also be served on the side as well, it makes a great texture addition to the meal.

This is a great lunch option because you can put individual servings in plastic containers and either refrigerate or freeze them for later use. Then when you need a quick lunch on the go, grab the container, throw it your lunch box and be on your way. If that works better for you, than you should really consider utilizing more recipes like these.

Grilled Cheese Keto Style

'Bread'

2 tablespoons almond flour

2 eggs

1 ½ tablespoons psyllium husk powder

2 tablespoons soft butter

½ teaspoon baking powder

Extras

1 tablespoon butter, soft

2 ounces of white or traditional cheddar

1. Combine the butter, almond flour, baking powder, and psyllium husk in a small bowl.
2. Stir this mixture together as much as you can, it will take the form of a very thick dough.

3. Add the 2 eggs and mix it together, you want your dough to be thick, so it seems too thin, keep mixing it together, as this will help thicken it up. This can take a full minute or more so be patient.

4. Scoop half the dough out into a square container roughly the size of a slice of bread, or the bottom a bowl to create bun, try to make sure it is spread evenly. You can also use a slightly larger container and cut in half later, if that is what you choose to do, use all the batter. Microwave this for a 90 to 100 seconds. Some might take a little longer to cook thoroughly so check it and it if it still too soft, microwave it for a little longer.

5. Gently remove it from the container by turning it upside down and tapping on the bottom of the container. If you used all of your batter you can cut it in half, if you need to repeat the process to create the other slice of bread, then do so.

6. Place the cheese in between the slices of bread.

7. In a pan set on medium heat add the butter and when it is hot add the sandwich. The bread will absorb the butter creating that delicious crisp, once it is golden brown, flip and cook the other side until golden brown.

8. Lastly, it is time to eat! A small side salad makes the perfect addition to this gooey, cheesy dish.

This is a great comfort food and probably one of the things that you will find yourself craving rather frequently. Again, just because you are on the ketogenic diet does not mean you have to give up everything you love, you just need to learn to make it in new and different ways that won't compromise ketosis.

Remember, this is a mix and match meal plan, you do not have to eat all the meals, but do try to keep an open mind. There is no lack of variety when it comes to the ketogenic diet, as a matter of fact, you can still have many of the foods you crave, they will just have a bit of a twist added to them. Whether or not you choose to make your lunches for the whole week or that day is up to you, but you do have the option. Keep in mind, this will get much easier the more you practice. In the beginning, the key is planning and sticking to it. If you need to create a weekly menu to keep you on track, then do it, there is nothing wrong with it. This is your diet and you have the right to do what works for you.

Chapter 5: Ketogenic Dinners

When it comes to dinners you can be a bit more creative because there isn't typically the need to grab it and go. Most people have more time to cook a dinner and not have to worry about making enough for a full week or whether or not it will travel well. Just like with the other recipes, you are going to choose your ingredients and keep track of the net carbohydrates you are consuming and since this is the last meal of the day, you will have a good idea of how many net carbohydrates you have let to devote to your dinner.

If you have a big dinner planned that you will use up more of your net carbohydrates than usual, make sure to limit your other meals and snacks throughout the day to give yourself the surplus you need for the special dinner. Try not to make this a habit, but everyone has some type of special occasion that requires a more elaborate dinner and this is still possible on the ketogenic diet, it just takes some extra planning. Here is a list of dinner recipes that are perfect for a ketogenic beginner.

Chicken with Creamy Greens

1 cup chicken stock

1 pound boneless chicken thighs, with skin still on

1 cup cream

2 cups dark leafy greens

2 tablespoons coconut oil

2 tablespoons coconut flour

2 tablespoons melted butter

1 teaspoon Italian herbs

Salt and pepper to taste

1. In a skillet set on medium high heat add the coconut oil. While this is getting hot, season the chicken with the salt and pepper, make sure to do both sides. When the oil is hot enough, brown the chicken on both sides

2. Continue to fry the chicken until it is crispy and cooked thoroughly. When you are cooking the chicken, you should also start making your sauce.

3. In a sauce pan melt the butter, when it stops sizzling, this means do not let it get brown, only melted, add the coconut flour and begin to whisk it together. Continue to whisk until it forms a thick paste.

4. Add the cream and increase the heat to bring it to a boil, continue to whisk. It will begin to thicken again and when it does, add the Italian herbs.

5. When your chicken is done frying, remove them from the stove and take out the thighs and set them aside.

6. Add the chicken stock into the skillet that just had the chicken in it and deglaze the skillet, slowly add the cream sauce and whisk. Slowly stir the greens into the sauce so they become evenly coated with the sauce.

7. Place the chicken on top of the greens and remove from the stove. You can now serve the meal, when dividing, it makes four servings.

Walnut Crusted Salmon

2 tablespoons sugar-free maple syrup

2, 3 ounce salmon fillets

½ cup walnuts

1 tablespoon olive oil

¼ teaspoon dill

½ tablespoon Dijon mustard

Salt and pepper to taste

1. Preheat oven to 350F.

2. Put all the walnuts in a food processor with the spices, mustard, and maple syrup. Blend this together until the consistency is very paste like.

3. In a skillet or pan heat up the olive oil until it is very hot, while this is happening dry both sides of the salmon, make sure to a do a good job. When the pan is very hot place the salmon in the pan skin down. Allow it to sear for three minutes.

4. While it searing, spoon the walnut mixture onto the fillets.

5. When they have finished being seared, place them on a pan or foil and place them in the oven to bake for around 8 minutes.

6. This is typically served on a bed of fresh spinach, but if you prefer other leafy greens, the choice is yours.

This is a quick and delicious dinner that will leave you feeling satisfied.

Crispy Baked Chicken Wings

3 pounds of wings

1 teaspoon baking soda

¼ cup of butter

1 tablespoon salt

2 teaspoons of baking powder

1. In a large plastic bag, dump in the salt, baking powder, baking soda, and all of the chicken wings.

2. Then shake the bag until all of the wings are coated in the mixture, try to make sure it is as even as possible.

3. Put all of the wings on a wire rack and leave in the refrigerator overnight, this will help them dry out which breaks the peptide bonds in the proteins.

4. The next day, preheat your oven to 450F and place the wings in the top middle rack, bake these for 20 minutes.

5. After the first 20 minutes, flip each wing over and bake for an additional 15 minutes or until they are as crispy as you like the,

6. To make a quick buffalo sauce mix together butter and hot sauce and toss them in this to make ketogenic buffalo wings. Enjoy!

This is a great dinner for when you have been watching your friends get their favorite wings from the local spot. When the craving for this type of comfort food hits you, now you can also enjoy them as well.

Stuffed Poblanos

1 tablespoon bacon fat

1 pound ground pork

½ onion

4 poblano peppers

7 baby bella mushrooms

1 teaspoon cumin

1 vine tomato

1 teaspoon chili powder

¼ cup chopped cilantro

Salt and pepper to taste

1. Rinse and prep all the vegetables, you want to mince garlic, slice the mushrooms and onions, and dice the tomatoes. If your cilantro is not already chopped, do this as well.

2. Set your oven to broil, while this is heating up, place the poblanos on a cookie sheet and put them in the oven when it is hot. Broil them for around 8 to 10 minutes, make sure to move them around every two minutes, you want consistent marks over the entire pepper. Then preheat your oven to 350F.

3. Using a paper towel or gloves to cover your fingers, carefully pull the skin from the peppers. Also, set the skin aside.

4. In a pan that is set on medium high-heat, begin to cook the pork, this is also where you add the bacon fat. Season with salt and pepper, but do not taste it until it has cooked all the way.

5. When it is browned you may now add the chili powder and cumin.

6. In the pan, slide all of the pork to one side and add the garlic and onions to the other side, you want them to be softened.

7. When those have softened add the mushrooms and mix all of it together, add more salt and pepper to suit your palate.

8. When the mixture starts to dry out a little add the tomatoes and cilantro.

9. Make a slice in the poblano pepper from the bottom to the stem and use a spoon or your fingers to remove the seeds. The seeds are spicy, so if you are sensitive to spicy foods, be sure to remove all of them.

10. Carefully fill each pepper with the pork mixture and bake them for around 8 to 10 minutes.

11. Remove them from the oven and they are now ready to serve!

These make a unique and fun dinner for what you are craving something simple and spicy. They will probably become a staple in your new diet if you enjoy spicier foods.

Coconut Shrimp

Shrimp

Egg whites from two eggs

1 pound shrimp, deveined and peeled

2 tablespoons coconut flour

1 cup coconut flakes, unsweetened

Chili Sauce

1 ½ tablespoon rice wine vinegar

1 diced red chili

½ cup apricot preserves, sugar-free

¼ red pepper flakes

1 tablespoon lime juice

1. If you are using frozen shrimp, make sure you thaw them out first, otherwise, if you bought them fresh peel and devein them if needed. Preheat your oven to 375F.

2. Put the egg whites in a bowl and beat them until soft peaks begin to form, this works best using a hand mixer, or if you are in a pinch, one beater inside a blender also works too.

3. In one bowl put the coconut flakes, in another the coconut flour. Take this time to also grease a cookie sheet.

4. Dip the shrimp in the flour, then dip them in the egg whites, and lastly, the flakes. Arrange them on the greased cookie sheet and bake them for about 15 minutes, make sure to flip them and broil for 3 to 5 more minutes.

5. To make the sauce simply add all the ingredients into a bowl mix them together. You might have some left over sauce, but it also goes well with chicken!

These are a great alternative to chicken nuggets or fried shrimp.

Dinners are generally the most fun part of ketogenic cooking because you can really experiment to find what pleases your palate. There are so many different recipes out there already, and you can tweak them so they work for your specific diet needs. Just remember, it might be overwhelming and difficult in the beginning, but you can do it. Just don't give up, let your body adjust and celebrate the small victories like the first pound lost or the first time you didn't have a carb craving all day. This will make the diet more fun and will help keep you motivated.

Chapter 6: Ketogenic Snacks

You are not locked in to only eating three meals a day with no snacking in between. Actually, you can graze a bit throughout the day if that works for you. However, not all snacks are created equal and some are much better than others. Just make sure not to let snacking get out of hand to the point that you are knocked out of ketosis because of it. Don't forget to add in the net carbohydrates from any of the snacks you have eaten throughout the day too, you want an authentic carbohydrate count and this will help make sure it is correct.

The best kind of snacks are the ones that you do not have to spend time preparing, and even though the ketogenic diet is best when you cook at home, there are some things that you can still just grab.

Ketogenic Snacks

Beef, pork, or chicken jerky

String Cheese

Seeds, sunflower, pumpkin, and chia

Pork rinds, just make sure to read the label, you can even dip them in ketogenic friendly dips such as Ranch or Bleu Cheese dressings.

Nut Butters, almond, coconut, and sunflower

Sugar-free jello

Cocoa nibs, this is the perfect alternative to a chocolate bar

In the beginning you might find yourself losing energy or getting hungry at weird times of the day, remember your body is learning to run on something new. So, this is completely normal. These snacks are easy to keep on hand and require no preparation. Just make sure to add them into your daily carbohydrate intake and they should help you during your transition to a low carbohydrate lifestyle.

It probably seems like this diet is overwhelming, but as soon as you get through the first couple of weeks and see the results, you will understand how beneficial it can really be. It will be difficult in the beginning, but you can and should stick it out. You will be proud of yourself in the end. So many people just like you have lost weight and enjoyed healthier lifestyles because of this diet. You don't want to let them reap all the benefits. So, don't let you, hold you back. The secret is finding what works for you and sticking to it, everyone works at their own pace and you are no exception. No matter how badly you might want to compare yourself to others, don't do it. Let your body go at the pace it is meant to, you will learn to know when it is okay to push yourself and when you have truly met your limits, but you won't know either of these until you dedicate

yourself and actually try.

PART III

Chapter 1: The Paleo Diet Benefits You

Backed Up With Science

Fad diets come and go, but the Paleo plan has been around for centuries and is not going anywhere. These are some of the benefits you will receive and the basis of how the information was acquired.

Benefit #1: *A Healthier Brain*: Evidence was provided by the University of Maryland Medical Center that Omega-e fatty acids, also known as polyunsaturated fatty acids {PUFAs}, play critical roles in your brain function. It also plays a major factor in healthy development and growth.

One of the best protein and fat sources comes from cold water fish, such as wild-caught salmon. The fish is packed with the omega-3 acids, which so many American diets are missing almost entirely. The DHA in the omega 3s is beneficial to the heart, eyes, and yes, the brain function!

Benefit #2: *Healthier Cells*: Harvard backs up the claim that your body depends on a healthy balance between the unsaturated and the saturated fats. That perfect balance is achieved through the Paleo diet.

Benefit #3: *The Rainbow Effect*: You are receiving all of your vitamins and minerals when you eat from the 'rainbow' of veggies. The *'Choose my Plate'* website can show you how it works. The dietary fiber, potassium, folic/folate acid, as well as the Vitamin A and C are part of the Paleo plan with its extensive array of menu plans.

Benefit #4: *Consume Unprocessed Foods*: You are eating a cleaner diet like your ancestors which is free from artificial ingredients and no preservatives. Wild caught and organic is preferable when possible.

Benefit #5: *Better 'Gut' Health*: Harvard has determined that the levels of cytokines, inflammatory messengers, are increased when a snack or meal is consumed with highly refined carbohydrates. These items would include white rice, white bread, soda, French fries, etc. You get the idea. Human-made fats and other elements can cause lots of inflammation in your intestinal tract. The result can be what is called 'leaky gut syndrome' which is what happens when stress is combined with the processed foods. This is one more reason the Paleo diet comes to the rescue.

Benefit #6: *Limitation of Fructose*: According to the National Center for Biotechnology, scientific proof exists with the testing from rodents which resulted in the high consumption of fructose. This high consumption can lead to high blood pressure, type 2 diabetes mellitus, obesity, as well as extra-hepatic and hepatic insulin resistance. Therefore, within the Paleo plan, you will notice some of the recipes will call for kiwi instead banana for this reason. The general rule-of-thumb is limiting yourself to about two to three pieces of fruit daily. It may also depend on your unique dietary needs. Now, let's get to cooking!

Chapter 2: Eye-Opening Breakfast Recipes

Cauliflower Wraps

These are the tastiest when served within a few hours of the baking time.

What about a quick Curry Wrap for breakfast?

Ingredients

2 eggs

½ head Cauliflower {cut into florets}

¼ teaspoon salt

½ teaspoon curry powder

What about a Garlic Herb Wrap?

Substitute ¾ teaspoon of dried herbs {thyme, oregano, basil or a combination}, and one minced clove of garlic in place of the curry powder.

Directions

1. Set the oven temperature to 375°F.

2. Cut some parchment paper to line two baking tins.

3. Use a food processor to pulse the cauliflower into a crumb-like texture.

4. Put them and ¼ cup of water into a pan with a tight-fitting top on the stovetop.

5. Cook for eight minutes on the medium-high heat setting.

6. Use a sieve to drain the cauliflower and place on a paper towel to remove all of the liquid.

7. Combine the remainder of the ingredients with the cauliflower mixture.

8. Shape two thin circles to form the wraps. Using a spatula; press down on the dough—making sure it stays on the paper.

9. Bake for 17 minutes. Place it on a wire rack to cool.

Serve as a scooper to pick up some light fillings or healthy dips.

Yields: Two Wraps

Bacon and Egg Breakfast Cups

Ingredients

4 strips chopped bacon

6 Original Sweet Rolls {King's Hawaiian}

Pepper and salt to taste

6 large Eggs {cage-free is best}

Directions

1. Preheat the oven temperature to 350°F. Prepare a muffin tin with some non-stick cooking spray.

2. Use a rolling pin {a wine bottle will work} to flatten the rolls. Next form them into the muffin tin along with some of the bacon bits and crack an egg over each of the tins.

3. Flavor with the pepper and salt.

4. Bake the concoction for approximately fifteen to seventeen minutes or until the egg whites are finished cooking according to your preference.

5. Garnish with some more bacon bits during the last five minutes of the baking cycle.

Cheddar Broccoli Egg Muffins

Ingredients
1 cup steamed/frozen – thawed box of broccoli
4 eggs
Pepper and salt
1/3 cup cheddar cheese {shredded & sharp}

Directions

1. Set the oven temperature in advance at 375°F.

2. Use some oil or cooking spray to coat six muffin tin holes.

3. Chop and add the broccoli into a bowl with the pepper, salt, and egg. Whisk and pour the ingredients into the tins—dividing the cheese equally.

4. Bake for twelve to fifteen minutes or until you see the eggs are firmly set.

Yields: Six Muffins

Sausage and Butternut Squash Frittata

This is a dish that is tasty for brunch, dinner, or anytime you have a craving!

Ingredients
3 Ounces crumbled/chopped sausage
1 tablespoon duck, bacon, or your choice of fat
¼ cup each:
- Butternut squash {Cubed and roasted}

- Diced red pepper

- Diced onion

Pepper and Sea Salt to taste
1/2 teaspoon dried herbs/2 teaspoons mixed fresh herbs
3 large eggs
Directions
1. Set the oven on the broiler function.

2. Whisk the herbs, pepper, salt, and eggs until well mixed.

3. Add the chosen fat to an ovenproof, ten-inch skillet. Sauté the peppers and

   onions for a few minutes until softened. Toss in the squash and sausage and

   heat thoroughly. Empty in the eggs and cook until the egg starts to cook

   around the edges.

4. Place the skillet in the oven and broil for three to five minutes.

Yields: Two Servings
Breakfast Hash with Yams
Ingredients
1 package thawed – frozen spinach/1 large bag fresh spinach
2 Sweet potatoes/yams
Eggs
Pepper and Salt
Chipotle Tabasco
Directions
1. Set the oven to 350°F.

2. Prepare the baking sheet. Use some cooking spray or use a silicon mat.

3. Arrange the potatoes; peeled & cut into ½-inch cubes—place them on the

   prepared sheet.

4. Bake for approximately 25 to 30 minutes. Turn one time about halfway

   through the cooking time.

Prep Time: Ten minutes
Cook Time: Twenty to thirty minutes
Yields: Six Servings
Paleo Oatmeal

Ingredients
3 Tablespoons coconut flour
½ Cup full-fat can coconut milk {plus ¼ cup water}
2 Tablespoons finely shredded coconut
½ banana mashed /1 egg
Toppings of your choice
Directions

1. Combine the coconut flour, liquid, and shredded coconut to pan on the

    stovetop—bringing it to a boil.

2. Lower the temperature setting and place a lid on the pan—simmer for about

    two to three minutes—stirring halfway through the cooking time.

3. Remove it from the heat and place the broken egg in the pan—quickly

    whisking so it cannot scramble. Put the pan back on the burner for about two

    more minutes to thicken. Enjoy.

Yields: One Serving

The Sweets Corner

Avocado Smoothie
Ingredients
14 ounces full-fat milk
2 chopped frozen bananas
1 cubed avocado
Directions

1. Combine each of the ingredients in a blender and mix until smooth. Enjoy!

Preparation Time: Five Minutes
Yields: Two Servings
Chocolate-Covered Strawberries Smoothie
Ingredients
½ Cup unsweetened strawberries {frozen}
¾ Cup {divided} skim milk
12 Large ice cubes {divided}
1 Pouch Rich Milk Chocolate {No Sugar Added} Carnation Breakfast Essentials
 Optional: 2 Tablespoons water
Directions
Preparation Layer 1: Place the strawberries on the first layer of the blender, four ice cubes, and ¼ cup of the milk. Pulse until the mixture is creamy smooth. Empty into a glass, and place in the freezer.
Preparation Layer 2:
Add the rest of the milk and the breakfast powder into the blender. Pulse until no lumps are remaining. Pour in the ice and pulse again.

Note: Use the water if the combinations are too thick.

Combination: Create your own masterpiece with the alternating layers. The ideas are endless!

Fruity Easter Egg - Smoothie

Ingredients

9 {divided} ice cubes

9 Tablespoons Water {divided}

9 Tablespoons Non-fat milk {divided}

½ Cup Each of Frozen:

- Blueberries

- Strawberries

- Pineapple

Directions

1. Duplicate the process for each one.

2. Add 3 Tablespoons of water, 3 Tablespoons of milk, and 3 ice cubes along with the fruit in the blender.

3. Pour each of the prepared ingredients into a glass and place it in the freezer and move on until you finish the three units.

4. To serve, alternate the three tasty glasses into a serving glass/glasses, and enjoy.

Yields: 2 Small or 1 large smoothie

Make as many as you wish and share with your friends and family!

Calories: 150

Mango Berry Smoothie Bowl

Ingredients

¾ Cup Almond milk

1 ripe {divided} banana

1 cup cubed frozen mango

Options:

- Ground Flax Seed

- Toasted coconut

- Frozen blueberries

- Frozen raspberries

Directions

1. Add the milk and ½ of the banana in the blender until smooth.

2. Toss in the mango and –again—blend until creamy smooth.

3. Pour it into your dish and top it off with the optional ingredients of your

    choice.

Yields: One Serving
Strawberry Shortcake Smoothie
Ingredients
¾ Cup Non-dairy or non-fat milk
1 Cup unsweetened frozen strawberries
1 teaspoon butter extract
Optional: Sweetener to taste
Use a blender and combine everything on the list; beginning with:

*   Strawberries

*   Milk

*   Butter extract

Serve and totally enjoy!
Banana Sushi
Ingredients
Your Favorite Nut Butter
1 Medium banana
Options:

*   Shredded coconut

*   Chia seeds

*   Chopped nuts

Directions

*   *Prepare the banana*: Peel, and spread the nut butter over the banana.

*   Sprinkle the desired toppings—pressing gently.

*   Cut them with a sharp knife into 'sushi' bites.

This 'odd' looking treat is a 'now or later' kind of treat for breakfast or any other time.
Freeze it if you want!
Preparation Time: Ten min.
Yields: One serving
Breakfast Cookies

Speaking of heaven; save this for a group of friends, so you are not tempted to eat all of them!

Ingredients
1 cup quick oats
2 bananas
1 teaspoon cinnamon

Directions
1. Set the oven temperature in advance to 350°F. Prepare a baking pan/sheet

   with a small amount of oil or some cooking spray.

2. Smash the bananas and stir in the oats. Toss in the cinnamon and stir.

3. Use a tablespoon to drop them onto the baking sheet, and bake for 15

   minutes.

Yields: 12 cookies {Serving size is one cookie with 10.5 carbs}

Pumpkin Bread

This dish is one of those treats that cannot be classified for just breakfast; it is good any time of the day or night!

Ingredients
¼ C. Coconut flour
2 tsp. cinnamon
1 C. blanched almond meal
1 tsp. baking soda
½ tsp. each:
- Nutmeg

- Baking powder

- Ground cloves

4 eggs
1 tsp. vanilla
1 C. pumpkin puree
¼ C. maple syrup
1 Tbsp. melted ghee/coconut oil

Directions
1. Preheat the oven to 375°F.

2. Prepare a loaf pan with some cooking spray/coconut oil.

3. Mix all of the dry ingredients in a mixing bowl.

4. Beat the eggs and add them into the dry ingredients.

5. Empty the batter into the prepared pan and bake for approximately 40 minutes.

Chapter 3: Time-Saving Lunches

Bacon – Pear & Walnut Salad with Pear Dressing

Ingredients for the Salad

1/3 Cup Walnuts

4 boiled eggs

1 Pear

5 ounces salad greens/favorite choice

4 slices bacon

Ingredients for the Dressing

¼ Cup olive oil

1 Peeled Pear

3 Tablespoons lemon or lime juice

Instructions

1. Prepare the eggs and cook the bacon, and lastly, dice the pear.

2. Arrange all of the ingredients for the dressing in the blender; mix well.

3. Toss the greens, bacon bits, diced pear pieces, and walnuts.

4. Combine all of the ingredients and top it off with the halved eggs.

Yields: Two Servings

Prep Time: Ten Min.

Cook Time: Twenty Min.

Antipasto Salad

Ingredients

4 Ounces each:

- Cubed pepperoni/salami

- Prosciutto cut into strips

1 large head/2 Romaine hearts romaine

½ Cup each

- Sweet or hot peppers {roasted or pickled}

- Mixed green and black olives

- Artichoke sliced hearts

Italian Dressing {to taste}

Directions

1. Blend all of the ingredients in a large salad serving dish.

2. Gently toss and drizzle with some Italian dressing.

Preparation Time: Ten Minutes

Avocado and Kale Salad

Ingredients
1 pitted avocado {flesh removed}
A medium bunch of Kale
1 Lemon {Juiced}
Directions
1. Use a large mixing dish and add all of the ingredients—tossing well.

2. Add a dash of pepper and salt for some flavoring.

Add other ingredients you might like.
Preparation Time: Five minutes
Egg Roll in a Bowl
Ingredients
1 Tablespoon unflavored coconut oil
1 small {sliced} head of cabbage
2 large carrots {sliced in long strips}
1/3 Cup coconut aminos
2 minced garlic cloves
Garnish: 4 Diced green onions
Optional: Shrimp or chicken {Protein of choice}
Directions
1. Use the med-high setting on the stovetop to melt the coconut oil and add the

   cabbage and carrots into a skillet.

2. Sauté until the veggies have softened. Add the sesame oil and coconut aminos.

3. Continue sautéing until more of the liquid/juices are absorbed. Toss in the

   garlic.

4. Add the onions to the top and enjoy.

You can always cook some tasty chicken for a side dish for lunch or dinner.
Zucchini Pasta Pesto
Ingredients
1 Cup cherry tomatoes
2/3 Cup Roasted garlic walnut pesto
2 large Zucchini
Sea salt
Garnish: Fresh basil
Note: You could use some pasta tongs, a colander, and veggie spiralizer or julienne for this recipe.
Directions
1. Rinse and drain the zucchini in a colander for about 20 minutes.

2. Use a julienne or spiralizer for the zucchini to provide the noodle part of the recipe, {the zoodles}.

3. Lightly salt the zucchini and toss with the tomatoes and pesto until well mixed.

4. Garnish with the basil.

Yields: Two to Four Servings
Asian Sesame Beef Salad
Ingredients for the Salad
½ Pound Beef {cut into cubes}
1 Tablespoon sesame oil
6 Ounces Iceberg lettuce {small pieces}
¼ Cup tamari sauce
2 Tablespoons each:
- Cilantro

- Green onions {chives or scallions}

- Sliced/whole almonds

¼ small shredded carrots
¼ shredded zucchini
1 Tablespoon Sesame Seeds
Cooking Oil: Avocado or Coconut for beef cubes
Ingredients for the Dressing
½ Tablespoon vinegar
1 ½ - Tablespoons olive/sesame oil
Directions
1. Pour the sesame oil and tamari sauce into a bowl.

2. Add the beef to the mixture for five minutes.

3. Slice the veggies and place them in a bowl

4. Sauté the beef in a skillet until done.

5. Toss it all together and add the dressing.

6. What a Treat!

Yields: Two Servings
Preparation Time: Ten minutes
Cooking Time: Twenty minutes
Chicken and Turkey
Chicken Salad with Walnuts and Grapes

Ingredients
2 Tablespoons each:
- Fresh lemon juice

- Minced shallot

¼ Cup olive oil
1 cup organic {halved & seedless} grapes
Fresh ground pepper and sea salt
2 cups diced & cooked chicken
½ Cup each:
- Diced organic celery

- Chopped walnuts

2 Tablespoons Fresh parsley {parsley}
Directions
1. Combine the lemon juice and shallots, and blend the oil in slowly. Flavor them

   with some pepper and salt.

2. Toss in the rest of the ingredients and enjoy!

Yields: Two Servings
Tacos with Chipotle Chicken
Ingredients
14.1 ounces skinless breasts {sliced into thin strips}
1 Red onion {finely sliced}
14.1 ounces whole or chopped tomatoes
1 Tablespoon chipotle in adobo sauce {finely chopped}
½ teaspoon cumin
Splash of olive oil {for frying}
Pinch of pepper, salt, and brown sugar
Fresh coriander leaves
Lettuce leaves
Sliced jalapeno chilies
Avocado slices or guacamole
Fresh tomatoes and spring onions {rustic salsa}
For Spritzing: Lime wedges
Directions
1) Add the oil to a skillet, and quick-fry the chicken until browned. Set to the

   side.

2) Add a splash of oil to the same pan and continue sautéing until the onion is

   soft.

3) Add the sugar, chipotle, tomatoes, and cumin--simmer for about 15 to 25 minutes; until the sauce becomes thickened around the pan's edges.

4) Arrange the products need to make the tacos using individual bowls. Give the chicken a lime spritz to kick-start the flavors.

Now that is healthy using the lettuce instead of a floured tortilla.
Prep. Time: Twenty minutes
Cook Time: Thirty minutes
Yields: Four Servings
Turkey Bacon Wrap
4 slices gluten-free deli turkey
1 head iceberg lettuce
4 slices gluten-free bacon
1 thinly sliced Roma tomato
1 thinly sliced avocado
Ingredients for the Basil-Mayo:
6 large – torn - basil leaves
½ Cup gluten-free mayonnaise {olive oil based is good}
1 chopped garlic clove
1 teaspoon lemon juice
Pepper and salt
Directions For the Mayonnaise
1. Use a food processor to combine all of the ingredients. First, the basil—then, the garlic.

2. Whisk everything together.

This mayo can be prepared a couple of days in advance.
Directions For the Wrap
1. Arrange two large leaves, a layer consisting of one slice of turkey, and a layer of the basil-mayo. Then; Layer turkey, bacon, avocado, and tomatoes. Add some pepper and salt for additional flavor.

2. Fold the bottom—then the sides—and roll like a burrito.

3. Cut it in half and enjoy.

Yields: 2 Wraps
Turkey – Raspberry & Avocado Salad
Ingredients
12 Ounces chopped - cooked turkey
¼ Cup walnut oil

1 Tablespoon each:
- Champagne vinegar

- Fresh lemon juice

1 teaspoon each:
- Honey

- Dijon mustard

Fresh ground pepper and sea salt {to taste}
1 Head-torn lettuce {Butter or Boston Bibb - awesome}
¼ Cup Toasted – roughly chopped walnuts
1 avocado
6 ounces organic raspberries
Directions
1. Prepare the avocado; cut it in half, pit, peel, and slice.

2. Combine the lemon juice, walnut oil, pepper, salt, honey, mustard, and vinegar

    in a jar with a tight-fitting lid. Shake the contents until thoroughly mixed.

3. Toss the avocado, turkey, and lettuce in a salad container. Drizzle with the

    dressing.

4. Top your creation off with some raspberries and walnuts and the remainder of

    the tasty dressing.

Yields: Two to Four Servings

Chapter 4: Fast-Paced Healthy Dinners

Grilled Lamb Chops

Enjoy these straight off of the grill!

Ingredients

2 Pounds Lamb chops

1 thinly sliced onion

2 Tablespoons olive oil

½ of a teaspoon freshly ground black pepper

¼ Cup distilled vinegar

1 Tablespoon minced garlic

2 teaspoons sea salt

Directions

1. Preheat the grill to med-hi.

2. Blend the olive oil, vinegar, pepper, salt, onion, and garlic in a Ziploc type of

   plastic bag; give it a good shake.

3. Add the chops, seal, and let it marinate in the fridge for one to two hours {no

   longer because it will become tough and too salty}.

4. Discard the remainder of the marinade and wrap the ends of the bones with

   some foil to prevent them from being burned on the grill.

5. Grill them for about three minutes for each side if you like the chops

   'medium.'

Yields: Six Servings

Preparation Time: Ten minutes

Cooking Time: Six Minutes

Beef

Mushroom Burgers

Ingredients

2 Tablespoons fresh chopped sage

¼ Pound mushrooms

3 cloves of garlic {pressed}

Fresh ground black pepper

4 Tbsp. {divided} olive oil

1 Pound lean ground beef

Directions

1. Set the oven temperature in advance to 350°F.

2. Wash and chop the mushrooms into quarter sections. Put them on a baking sheet and bake until they are reduced in size by half, usually for 15 to 20 minutes.

3. Bring the oil to medium heat in a skillet with the sage and garlic for about three minutes. Place the mushrooms and the mixture into a processor until they are in small pieces. Add the beef and pulse to combine the burger mix.

4. Make the patties and add the remainder of the oil to the skillet; cook for about five minutes for each side.

You can also prepare these on an outdoor or indoor grill.

Beef Ragu

Ingredients

¼ Cup red pesto

1.8 Pounds {28.2 Ounces} Ground Beef

1 Tbsp. Butter or ghee

½ tsp. pink Himalayan salt {more or less}

2 to 4 Tablespoons fresh chopped parsley

Serve with some 'zoodles.'

Directions

1. Put the meat into a hot skillet with the butter/ghee {save some butter for the zoodles}.

2. Cook until it is browned, around five minutes should be sufficient. Toss in the salt, parsley, and pesto; continue cooking about three to five more minutes.

3. When the meat is finished cooking, move it into a dish.

4. *Make the Zoodles:* Zoodles are merely four medium zucchini {one per serving}. You make them using a vegetable spiralizer or julienne peeler. Add the inner core to the zoodles.

5. Add the zoodles to the meat and cook for about two to five minutes.

6. Turn off the heat and serve.

Yields: Four Servings
Chicken and Turkey
Barbecue Stuffed Sweet Potatoes
Ingredients
1 Pound Chicken Breasts {Cooked & skinless}
2 halved – medium sweet potatoes
1/3 cup barbecue sauce – your choice {more or less}
Optional Garnish: Sliced Green onions or chopped parsley
Directions
1. Heat the oven to 425°F.

2. Shred the chicken.

3. Place the potatoes cut-side up on a baking pan. Roast for about 35 minutes

   according to the size of the potatoes.

4. Use the medium-low setting and blend the chicken with the barbecue sauce in

   a saucepan for about five to ten minutes.

5. Top each of the potatoes with a scoop of chicken and garnish with your

   preferences.

Yields: Four Halves
Chili Roasted Chicken Thighs
Ingredients
2 Pounds Chicken thighs {boneless}
1 Tbsp. Olive oil
Fresh ground pepper and Sea Salt
1 Tbsp. Chili powder
Optional: Fresh cilantro for garnish
Lime wedges for serving
Directions
1. Heat the oven in advance to 375°F.

2. Arrange the chicken on a baking sheet with a rim.

3. Drizzle it with the oil and give each of the thighs a rub with the pepper, salt,

   and chili powder.

4. Roast the thighs for about 15 minutes.

5. Sprinkle some of the cilantro on them and serve with a lime wedge or two.

Yields: Four Servings
Crock Pot Chicken
Ingredients
1 {3 to 5 Pounds}Chicken
Suggested Options:

- Paprika

- Garlic

- Olive oil

- Rosemary

Directions
1. Remove the chicken from the package—making sure you remove all of its 'innards' as well as any fat. Rinse and pat the entire chicken dry with a paper towel. Place it in the cooker breast side down.

2. Throw the paper towels away and wash your hands.

3. Give the bird a drizzle of olive oil and a dab with the garlic cloves or rosemary.

4. Turn on the cooker using the low setting for seven hours {more or less}. It should be 165°F if tested with a meat thermometer.

5. Add some peas and potatoes for a delicious meal.

Indian Style Chicken Drumsticks
Ingredients
2 to 3 Tbsp. Salt
3 to 4 Tbsp. garam masala
10 Chicken Drumsticks
Directions
1. Heat the oven to 450°F.

2. Use some coconut oil to grease a large baking tray.

3. Combine the garam masala and salt in a dish.

4. Pat the drumsticks dry with a paper towel. Coat them with the mixture and arrange on the prepared tray. Try not to let them touch so that they will cook evenly.

5. Bake for forty minutes.

Yields: Five Drumsticks per Serving {Two Servings}
Preparation Time: Five minutes
Cooking Time: Forty minutes
Italian Dressing Grilled Chicken Breasts
Ingredients
½ Cup Paleo Italian dressing {see below}
4 Chicken breasts {boneless}
Directions
1. Use a shallow glass dish to marinate the breasts for a minimum of 30 minutes;

   turning once.

2. Set the grill to the medium-high setting. Grill the chicken for three to five

   minutes on each side. The internal temperature should reach 155°F when it is

   done.

Yields: Four Servings
Ingredients For the Italian Dressing:
1 minced garlic clove
1 teaspoon dried oregano
1 Tablespoon flat leaf parsley {or your choice}
¼ teaspoon fresh ground black pepper
½ teaspoon sea salt {more or less}
¾ Cup olive oil
¼ Cup red wine vinegar
Directions for the Italian Dressing
1. Mix all of the ingredients and add them into a tight-fitting jar.

2. Shake the components until they are well mixed.

3. Make any 'taste' adjustments and serve.

Yields: About one cup
Chicken Tenders
Ingredients
1 Pound skinless chicken breast cut into strips
½ Cup Almond Meal
¾ teaspoon paprika
¼ teaspoon ground cumin seed
½ teaspoon salt
¼ teaspoon ground coriander seed
1 egg {beaten}
Directions
1. Prepare a baking sheet with a layer of parchment paper.

2. Set the oven temperature to 425°F.

3. In a shallow dish, combine all of the spices and the almond meal.

4. Break and beat the egg into a separate shallow container.

5. Use some paper towels to pat the chicken dry. Dip it into the egg first, and then the almond mixture—making sure to coat all of the sides evenly.

6. Bake and turn once about midway of the cooking cycle to ensure even temperature ranges which should be 180°F when the tenders are ready.

Yields: Four Servings
Preparation Time: Ten minutes
Cooking Time: Sixteen to eighteen minutes
Roasted Turkey Breast
Ingredients
2 {2-3 Pounds} Bone-in Turkey Breast halves
Freshly ground pepper
Sea salt {coarsely ground}
2 Tablespoons melted duck fat
Directions
1. Heat the oven to 425°F.

2. Arrange the turkey, skin-side up in a baking pan with some rimmed edges.

3. Rub the turkey with the duck fat. Place it in the oven and lower the heat to 375°F.

4. Bake until the internal temperature is 165°F or about 1-1 ½ hours.

5. Cover the turkey with some aluminum foil and let it rest for about fifteen minutes before slicing for dinner.

Yields: Four to Six Servings

Soups and Stock
Asparagus Soup {Gluten-free}
Ingredients
1 small chopped shallot
1 pound asparagus {trimmed}
1 Tablespoon butter/ghee
Pepper and salt {to taste}
2 Cups chicken stock {see recipe below}

Directions

1. Prepare the shallots using a pinch of salt and the butter/ghee in a pan for

    about five minutes, or until softened.

2. Add the chicken stock and asparagus, bringing the mixture to a boil. Lower the

    heat and simmer for approximately five minutes.

3. Add the product to a blender/mixer, and process until the desired consistency

    is reached. Flavor the soup with the pepper and salt.

Yields: Two Servings

Chicken Stock {Crock-Pot®}

You never know when you are going to need some fresh chicken stock. Here is one you need to remember.

Ingredients

1 medium {quartered} onion
1 chicken carcass
3 quartered celery stalks
3 quartered carrots
Water to cover the chicken
1 Tablespoon apple cider vinegar

Directions

1. Add all of the components for the stock into a slow cooker/crock pot.

2. Strain the final product and freeze or refrigerate.

Cook Time: 12 to 18 hours

Fish

Cajun Cod Filet and Chips

Ingredients

Pacific Cod {wild-caught preferred}
Coconut Oil
Cajun Seasoning

Directions

1. Prepare a large skillet over medium heat with a couple of tablespoons of

    coconut oil.

2. Cover the filets with all of the seasonings and cook on each side for two to

    three minutes.

3. Take the fish off of the heat and let it rest for two to three minutes.

4. Serve with a sprinkle of fresh lime juice.

5. The ideas are endless from here.

For the Sweet Potato Chips
Ingredients
3 cups coconut oil
5 medium sweet potatoes
1 teaspoon pepper
2 teaspoons sea salt
Directions
1. Peel the potatoes and slice them thin.

2. Give them a shake or two of salt and pepper

3. Drop the potatoes into a skillet with the oil.

4. When done cooking; absorb the grease with some paper towels.

Complement any dish with this treat.

Mustard Crusted Salmon & Roasted Asparagus
Ingredients
8 ounces asparagus
2 {6-ounce} salmon fillets
1 Tablespoon garlic infused olive oil
2 Tablespoons whole grain mustard
Fresh ground black pepper
Salt
Lemon slices
Instructions
1. Use some parchment paper to line a rimmed baking sheet.

2. Set the oven in advance to 400°F.

3. Arrange the asparagus on one end and the salmon on the other.

4. Use some olive oil to drizzle the asparagus, lightly tossing.

5. Flavor with some pepper and salt.

6. Spread the mustard on the fish top.

7. Bake for about 10 minutes and garnish with the lemon.

Yields: Two Servings

Pork
The Weekender {Crock-Pot®}

Ingredients
2 Pounds Pork Loin
3 Tablespoons coconut oil
2 Tablespoons lemon juice
1 {6-8 -ounce} tomato paste
1 seeded jalapeno pepper
1 chopped onion
2 teaspoons chili powder
4 minced garlic cloves
1 teaspoon each:
- Thyme

- Cumin

½ teaspoon each:
- Paprika

- Cayenne pepper

Directions
1. Dump everything into a slow-cooker pot and set it on low for 5 hours.

2. Once the cooking cycle is completed; use two forks and shred the pork.

Grilled Pork Chops with Pineapple Salsa
Ingredients for the Salsa
4 Organic boneless pork chops
¼ Cup olive oil
2 Tablespoons honey
¼ Cup fresh lime juice
1 teaspoon chipotle chili flakes
¼ teaspoon:
- Pepper

- Sea salt

1 recipe *Grilled Pineapple Salsa*
Directions
1. Mix the pepper, salt, lime juice, chipotle flakes, honey, and olive oil. Empty the

   contents over the chops—tossing to saturate thoroughly. Marinate for one

   hour

2. Grill the pineapple for the salsa and add the chops to cook for three to five

   minutes for each side. It is ready when the internal temperature reaches 145°F.

3.   Let the meat rest for three minutes and top with the salsa.

Yields: Four Servings
For the Grilled Salsa
¼ Cup finely diced onion
1 ½ Cups diced - grilled pineapple
1 finely diced jalapeno
¼ cup fresh – chopped cilantro
Sea salt to taste
Juice of 1 lime
Directions for the Salsa
   1.   Add everything in one bowl and toss to combine

   2.   Adjust the seasonings to your liking. Enjoy!

Chapter 5: Snacks, Appetizers, and Desserts

Granola – Walnut and Cranberry

Ingredients

2 C. chopped walnuts

1 C. each

- Unsweetened shredded coconut

- Silvered almonds

- Raw pumpkin seeds

2 Tablespoons melted coconut oil

¼ teaspoon salt

3 Tablespoons honey

1 C. dried cranberries {apple juice sweetened}

Directions

1. Set the oven to 300°F. Prepare a rimmed cookie sheet with some parchment paper.

2. Mix the salt, nuts, coconut, and seeds in a large container.

3. Blend in the honey and coconut oil until thoroughly mixed.

4. Bake for 28 to 20 minutes and add the dried cranberries.

Let the granola chill before serving.

Yields: Six Cups {approximately}

Bacon Wrapped Pears {Appetizer}

Ingredients

8 Slices bacon

2 Pears

Directions

1. Heat the temperature in the oven to 400°F.

2. Prepare a baking sheet with a rim using some aluminum foil.

3. Leave the skin on the pears, but cut them into quarters.

4. Use one slice of bacon for each quarter.

5. Bake until the bacon is crispy; about thirty minutes.

6. Garnish with a few fresh herbs of your choice.

Preparation Time: Ten Minutes
Cooking Time: Thirty Minutes
Roasted Shrimp Cocktail
1 Pound Uncooked Shrimp
Paleo Cocktail Sauce {recipe below}
Pepper and Sea Salt
1 Tablespoon Olive oil
Lemon wedges
Paleo Cocktail Sauce Ingredients:
2 Tablespoons organic tomato paste
1 Cup organic strained tomatoes
¼ Cup + 1 Tablespoon prepared horseradish
½ teaspoon sea salt
1 tablespoon fresh lemon juice
1.   Combine them all.

Yields: 1 ½ Cups
Directions for the Shrimp
1.   Heat the oven in advance to 425°F.

2.   Toss the shrimp with the oil, pepper, and salt.

3.   Use a rimmed baking sheet and place the shrimp on it in a single layer.

4.   Turn them once during the five to ten minutes it will take for the shrimp to

turn pink. It varies because of the size of the shrimp.

5.   Garnish with the Paleo cocktail sauce and lemon wedges.

Yields: Four Servings
This treat is perfect for a special evening or just because you deserve it!
Sprout Chips
Ingredients
1 Pound Brussels Sprouts
Sea Salt
2 teaspoons Olive oil
Directions
1.   Set the oven temperature to 350°F.

2.   Using a paring knife, remove the bottom of the sprouts, so the leaves will

come apart.

3.   Put the leaves in a bowl and give them a drizzle of oil, and arrange them on a

baking sheet.

4.   Bake them for approximately four to six minutes.

5.   {Watch them like a hawk, so they don't burn.}

Preparation Time is 10 minute
Cook Time: 5 minutes

Index
Chapter 2: Eye-Opening Breakfast Recipes

- Cauliflower Wraps

- Bacon and Eggs Breakfast Cups

- Cheddar Broccoli Egg Muffins

- Sausage and Butternut Squash Frittata

- Breakfast Hash with Yams

- Paleo Oatmeal

The Sweets Corner

- Avocado Smoothie

- Chocolate-Covered Strawberries Smoothie

- Fruity Easter Egg Smoothie

- Mango Berry Smoothie Bowl

- Strawberry Shortcake Smoothie

- Banana Sushi

- Breakfast Cookies

- Pumpkin Bread

Chapter 3: Time-Saving Lunches

- Antipasto Salad

- Avocado and Kale Salad

- Egg Roll in a Bowl

- Zucchini Pasta Pesto

- *Serve with some 'zoodles.'*

- Asian Sesame Beef Salad

Chicken and Turkey
- Chicken Stock {Crock-Pot®}

- Chicken Salad with Walnuts and Grapes

- Tacos with Chipotle Chicken

- Turkey Bacon Wrap

- Turkey – Raspberry & Avocado Salad

Chapter 4: Fast-Paced Healthy Dinners

- Grilled Lamb Chops

Beef
- Mushroom Burgers

- Beef Ragu

Chicken
- Barbecue Stuffed Sweet Potatoes

- Chili Roasted Chicken Thighs

- Crock Pot Chicken

- Indian Style Chicken Drumsticks

- Italian Dressing Grilled Chicken Breasts

- *Ingredients For the Italian Dressing*

- Chicken Tenders

- Roasted Turkey Breast

Soups and Stock
- Chicken Stock {Crock-Pot®}

Fish
- Cajun Cod Fillet and Chips

- *For the Sweet Potato Chips*

- Mustard Crusted Salmon & Roasted Asparagus

Pork
- The Weekender {Crock-Pot®}

- Grilled Pork Chops with Pineapple Salsa

- Pineapple Salsa Recipe

Chapter 5: Snacks, Appetizers, and Desserts

- Granola – Walnut and Cranberry

- Bacon Wrapped Pears {Appetizer}

- Roasted Shrimp Cocktail and Cocktail Sauce

- Sprout Chips

PART IV

Chapter 1: The Power of the Crock Pot and Its Benefits

The Ways You Can Benefit

Think of how many times you have experienced 'spells' that you did not feel like spending hours over the stove preparing dinner. Can you relate? How about the times during the holidays when you are planning on a houseful of guests; yikes? By the way, "Don't sweat it because you have your fabulous cooker and all of these new recipes to try out."

These are a few ways to make the path a bit easier:

Get Ahead of the Meal: Preparing food with your Crock-Pot® can put you ahead of the game the night before you have a busy day planned. You can always make the meal for the next day in just a few minutes. Put all of the ingredients (if they can combine overnight) into the pot, so when you get up the next morning; all you need to do is take it out of the fridge, and let it get to room temperature. Turn it on as you head out of the door and dinner will be ready when you get home. YES!

Save a lot of Effort and Time: All it takes is a few good recipes and a little bit of your valuable time. In most of the cases, these recipes are geared towards a fast lifestyle and will be ready with just a few simple steps. After some time and practice, you will know exactly which ones will be your favorites; all of them!

Cut Back on Dining Out: Having an enjoyable meal at home is so much more personal for your family because you (and your pot) prepared it! Not only that, You will eliminate the temptation to order foods that might not be so healthy and in turn—will be more expensive.

Watching the Extra Liquids: There is no need to use additional ingredients, other than what is described within each of the recipes. Ideally, you should not fill the more than half to two-thirds full of ingredients. Too much liquid will cause a leakage from the top and may result in improperly cooked food.

Cook it Slow & Leave it Alone: A slow cooker is known for creating delicious dishes while bringing out all of the natural flavors. So, go ahead and go to work or have some fun—

or—better yet go to bed early! There is no need to worry about checking on it (unless the recipe calls for it). Each time the lid is removed—valuable heat is escaping—resulting in a breakdown of the advised times. Just keep that element it in mind, even though it smells so good!

Trimming the Fat: One huge advantage to the use of this type of cooking is you can save quite a chunk of money purchasing cheaper cuts of meat. Also, capitalize on the flavorful meat in small quantities and by bulking up on veggies with smaller meat portions.

Hot Antioxidants

Many recent studies have discovered cooking some food items such as tomatoes will increase the bioavailability of many of the nutrients. For example, lycopene which is linked to cancer and heart prevention becomes move available to the body because the heat releases the lycopene.

A study from 2003 compared the content of fresh, frozen, and canned corn which was processed with heat; specifically lutein and xeaxanthin, and found less lutein in the fresh version. This lutein is mostly well-known to protect you from some eye diseases. Score 'ONE' for the Crock-Pot®.

Who Knew?

Basic Times & Settings

The question always arises of how long you should cook your items if you don't have a recipe for a Crock-Pot®. These are only general guidelines because the size of a pot will make a difference in the cooking times.

Regular Cooking Times	Crock Pot® High Temperatures	Crock Pot® Low Pot Temperatures
Hours		
1/4 to 1/2	1 to 2	4 to 6
1/2 to 1	2 to 3	5 to 7
1 to 2	3 to 4	6 to 8
2 to 4	4 to 6	8 to 12

Note: You must consider that root veggies take longer than other vegetables and meats which mean they should be placed in the lower part of the pot.

Are You Ready? Of course, you are!

Chapter 2: Healthy Breakfast Recipes

Boiled Eggs

Did you ever wake up in the middle of the night for a 'potty' break, and decided you want some boiled eggs or egg salad for breakfast or work tomorrow, but do not have the time to sit around and wait for the eggs to cook? You have a cure for that!
Ingredients and Instructions
The simplicity is amazing!

1) Pour some water into the Crock-Pot®, add as many eggs as you

   want, and set the pot for 3 ½ hours on the low setting. Go back

   to bed and enjoy tomorrow!

One-Hour Bread

Crave that fresh bread—no longer! You can have some delicious comfort food shortly!
Ingredients
1 ½ C. Baking Mix
3 Tbsp. Italian Seasoning
½ cup milk (skim is okay)
Optional: ½ C. shredded cheese or 3 Tbsp. Grated Parmesan cheese
Directions

1) Prepare the cooker with some non-stick cooking spray.

2) Combine all of the ingredients until the lumps are gone and

   empty into the cooker.

3) *Notes:* Bisquick® is a good choice.

Breakfast Fiesta Delight
Directions
1 Pound Country-Style Sausage
1 Package (28-ounces) frozen hash brown potatoes (thawed)
½ Cup whole milk
12 large eggs
1 ½ Cups shredded Mexican blend cheese
Directions

1) Prepare the Crock-Pot® by spraying it with some cooking spray

   to help with the cleanup.

2) Brown and crumble the sausage in a frying pan; remove and pat the grease away using a paper towel.

3) Whip the eggs together in a mixing container.

4) Layer the ingredients with a layer of potatoes, cheese, sausage, and eggs.

5) *Serving Time*: Have some salsa, sour cream, pepper, and salt for a tasty topping.

Servings: Six to Eight
Prep Time is fifteen minutes
Cooking Time is six to eight hours.

Italian Sausage Scramble

Ingredients
1 ½ Lbs. Italian sausage
1 medium yellow onion
6 medium red potatoes
¼ Cup fresh Italian minced parsley
One medium diced tomato
1 Cup frozen/fresh kernel corn
2 cups grated Cheddar cheese

Directions

1) Discard the outer casing from the sausage. Peel and dice the onions and potatoes.

2) Sauté the onion and crumbled sausage until browned. Place them on a few paper towels to absorb the grease/fat and add the items to the slow cooker.

3) Combine the rest of the ingredients—blending well. Cover and cook.

Servings: Six

Prep Time is 15 Minutes.

Cook Time: The high setting is for four hours, and the lower setting is for six to eight hours.

The Sweeter Side of Breakfast

Blueberry Steel Cut Oats

Ingredients

1 ½ C. of water

2 C. frozen blueberries

1 banana

1 C. Steel cut oats

1- ½ C. Vanilla almond milk

1 Tbsp. butter

1 ½ tsp. cinnamon

Directions

1) Prepare a six-quart cooker with the butter, making sure to cover the sides also.

2) Mash the banana slightly and add all of the ingredients into the Pot—stirring gently.

3) Place the top on the crock pot and cook for *one hour* on the HIGH setting; switch to the WARM setting overnight, and sleep tight!

Wake up ready for a busy day by adding a drizzle of honey and get moving!

Servings: Four to Six

Preparation Time: Fifteen Minutes

Cooking Time: Eight hours

Pumpkin Pie Oatmeal

Ingredients

1 C. oats (steel cut)

3 ½ C. water

1 C. pumpkin puree

¼ tsp. each:

- salt

- vanilla extract

- pumpkin pie spices

Optional: 2 Tbsp. maple syrup
Directions

1) Use some non-stick cooking spray to coat the Crock-Pot®.

2) Empty the oats into the Pot.

3) Mix the remainder of the ingredients in a large mixing container, and pour over the oats.

4) *Note:* If you like sweeter oatmeal just adjust the flavor after it is cooked.

Cooking Time: Eight hours on low

Pumpkin Butter

Ingredients
4 Cups pumpkin
1 tsp. ground ginger
2 tsp. cinnamon
1-¼ Cups honey/maple syrup
½ tsp. nutmeg
1 tsp. vanilla extract (*optional*)
Instructions

1) Blend the vanilla, syrup/honey, and pumpkin puree in the Crock-Pot®.

2) Cover and cook. During the last hour—add the ginger, cinnamon, and nutmeg.

3) If you want it a little thicker, you can crack the lid. After all, the aroma is tantalizing—especially first thing in the morning!

You can store in jars in the bottom of the fridge for a healthy addition—anytime.
Yields: About 10 ounces
Preparation Time: Five Minutes
Cooking Time: Five hours

Chapter 3: Time-Saving Lunch Specialties

Beef Tacos

Ingredients

1 Package taco seasoning

1 (ten-ounce) Can tomatoes and green chilies (Rotel)

1 Pound lean ground beef

Directions

1) Add everything listed into your Crock-Pot®.

2) If you are available; stir every couple of hours to break up the

   beef or break it up before serving.

3) Serve on a floured tortilla or taco shell with your choice of

   toppings.

Servings: 12 tacos

Preparation Time: Two Minutes

Cooking Time: Five to Six Hours

Root Beer & BBQ Chicken

Ingredients

1 (18-ounce) bottle barbecue sauce

4 chicken breasts

¼ teaspoon each pepper and salt

½ can or bottle root beer (full-sugar)

Note: You can use Dr. Pepper or Coke instead of root beer.

Directions

1) Pour the drink of choice, and place the chicken in the cooker.

2) Drain once the chicken has finished cooking, and discard most of

   the liquid—but leaving enough to prevent dryness.

3) Flavor with some pepper and salt if desired and empty the

   contents of the sauce into the Crock-Pot®, cooking for about 15

   to 20 minutes.

4) Enjoy on some burger buns or rolls.

Cooking Time: The high temperature will have it ready in 3 hours.

Stuffed Banana Peppers

Ingredients
1 Package Italian Sausage
Banana Peppers
2 Jars of Marinara Sauce (approximately)
Directions

1) Adapt this for your crowd on the amounts used.

2) Remove both ends of the peppers and scoop out the seeds and discard them.

3) Pour ½ of the jar of sauce in the Crock-Pot®.

4) Dice the sausage, in case it is not already prepared.

5) Stuff the pepper with the sausage and put them into the Pot.

6) Pour the sauce over the banana peppers.

Cooking Time: Low for eight to nine hours

Crock-Pot® Taco Soup

Ingredients
1 (14.5-ounces) Can Each:

- Beef broth

- Petite diced tomatoes

1 (15-ounces) Can Each:

- Black beans

- Corn

1 (10-ounces) Can Rotel Original
1 Can kidney beans (16-ounces)
1 (1-oz.) pouch each:

- Taco seasoning mix

- Ranch seasoning mix (Hidden Valley)

½ teaspoon salt
1 ½ teaspoons onion powder
1 Lb. ground beef
Garnish: Sour Cream, Fritos, chopped green onions, or some shredded cheddar cheese
Notes: The recipe is excellent if you choose the 'Diced Tomatoes with Green Chilies.'
Directions

1) Cook the beef and drain. Rinse and drain all of the cans of

   veggies except for the chilies; reserve the liquid from the corn

   and tomatoes.

2) Toss everything into the Crock-Pot® (except for the garnishes).

3) Cook for the necessary time.

4) When the process is completed, add the garnishes of your choice

   with some Fritos on the side to complement the flavors

Servings: 8 to 10
Prep Time: Ten minutes
Cook Time: Low for 4 hrs. or High for 2 hrs.

Chapter 4: Dinner in a Hurry
Beef
Meat for the Tacos
Ingredients
2 Lbs. Ground beef (lean)
1 cup diced onions/Birds Eye Chopped Onions and Garlic
1 Package low-sodium taco seasoning mix
Directions

1) Put the burger into the Crock-Pot® and cook it for four to six

   hours. If you are in the area of the kitchen—stir the meat every

   couple of hours to ensure it is cooking evenly (if not—no

   worries).

2) When the cooking cycle is complete; drain the beef on some

   paper towels.

3) Combine the onions and ½ to one package of the taco seasoning.

4) Blend well and continue cooking for about one more hour

Servings: Six
Preparation Time: Five Minutes
Cooking Time: Low setting: Four to Six hours
Steak Pizzaiola
Ingredients
1 (one to two pounds) London Broil
1 Yellow, orange, or red sliced bell pepper
1 Large sliced onion
¼ Cup water
½ to ¾ of a jar (your choice) tomato pasta sauce
Directions

1) Flavor the meat with the pepper and salt and place it into the

   Crock-Pot®.

2) Add the peppers and onions, followed by your favorite sauce,

3) Cook for six to eight hours. (Flip a time or two if you are home.)

4) Serve over some pasta, potatoes, or veggies.

Cooking Time: Low heat for six to eight hours
Steaks in the Pot
Ingredients
4 to 6 steaks
¼ C. White Wine
2 T. A-1 Sauce
2 T. Dijon mustard
Directions
1) Blend the mustard and steak sauce; add it to each of the pieces of

steak.

2) Add the meat into the Crock-Pot®, add the wine, and cook for

six to eight hours.

Servings: Four or More
Cooking Time: 6 to 8 Hours on the low setting

Chicken and Turkey
Buffalo Chicken
Ingredients
3 to 5 Pounds (no skin or bones) chicken breasts
1 (12-ounce) Bottle Red Hot Wings Buffalo Sauce
1 Pouch ranch dressing mix
Directions
1) Put the chicken into the Crock-Pot®. Empty the sauce over the

breasts and sprinkle the ranch mix over the top. Cover and

Cook.

2) Take the chicken out of the Pot and throw away the sauce.

3) Shred the chicken with a couple of forks. It should be tender.

4) Put it back into the cooker and stir to coat the chicken

thoroughly.

5) Leave it in the pot on low about one more hour. Most of the sauce will be absorbed.

Cooking Time: Low for five hours

Caesar Chicken

Ingredients
1 bottle (12-ounces) Caesar dressing
4 skinless & boneless chicken breasts
½ Cup shredded Parmesan cheese

Directions

1) Add the breasts of chicken to the Crock-Pot®.

2) Cook the chicken for the specified time and drain the juices.

3) Empty the dressing over the breasts.

4) Sprinkle the cheese on top of that and cook for thirty more minutes covered until done.

Have a side of Caesar salad to complement the meal.

Servings: Four
Prep Time: 5 minutes
Cooking Time: Use the low setting for 6 hrs. ; the high setting High for 3 hrs.

Cranberry Chicken

Ingredients
4 (no skin or bones) Chicken Breasts
1 (8-ounces) bottle Kraft Catalina dressing
1 Pouch dry onion soup
1 (14-ounces) Can Ocean Spray Whole Cranberry Sauce

Directions

1) Cook the chicken in the Crock-Pot® according to your specified times. Drain the juices.

2) Combine the cranberry sauce, onion soup mix, and dressing. Empty it over the chicken.

3) Cook—covered—about 30 minutes.

Servings: Four

Preparation Time: Five minutes
Cooking Time: High for three hours or low for six hours
French Onion Chicken
Ingredients
4 Chicken breasts (no bones or skin)
1 Can French Onion soup (10.5-ounces)
½ cup sour cream
Directions

1) Put the breasts in the Pot and cook for the stated time. Empty

   the liquids.

2) Combine the soup and sour cream and add into the pot on top of

   the chicken

breasts.

3) Cook covered for about 30 minutes.

Servings: Four
Preparation Time: Five Minutes
Cooking Time: The high setting will take approximately three hours, whereas the low setting takes six hours.
Hawaiian Chicken
Ingredients
4 to 5 skinless and boneless breasts of chicken (thawed)
1 (20-oz.) Can Dole Pineapple Chunks
1 Bottle (12-oz.) Heinz Chili Sauce
1/3 C. brown sugar
Directions

1) Cook the chicken until its predetermined time limit is completed.

   Empty the liquid.

2) Combine the brown sugar, ½ of the juices of the can of

   pineapples, the chili sauce, and the chunks of pineapple.

3) Empty the mixture over the drained breasts and heat on the high

   setting for approximately 30 minutes or so.

4) Have a bit of pineapple in every bite. Yummy!

Servings: 4 to 5
Preparation Time: 5 min.
Cooking Time: High = 6 hrs. / Low = 3 hrs.

Honey Mustard Chicken

Ingredients
1 (12-ounces) Bottle Dijon mustard
1/3 C. honey
4 skinless & boneless chicken breasts (thawed)

Directions

1) Cook the chicken for its predetermined time and dispose of the

   juices.

2) Combine the mustard and honey in a small dish.

3) Empty the sauce over the chicken and cook for about ½ hour

   (covered) until done,

Servings: Four
Preparation Time: Five Minutes
Cooking Time: Use the low setting for six hrs. Or on high for three hrs.

Chicken Italian Style

Ingredients
4 chicken breasts (thawed – no bones- no skin)
1 (16-ounce) Bottle Italian Dressing

Directions

1) Place the breasts of chicken into your Crock-Pot® and pour the

   dressing on them.

2) Put the lid on and let it do your work!

Servings: Four
Preparation Time: 5 minutes
Cooking Time: Use the high setting to prepare the chicken for 3.5 hrs. Or use the low setting for 7 hours.

Swedish Meatballs

Ingredients
1 (12-ounce) jar Heinz HomeStyle Gravy (Savory Beef)
1 (eight-ounce) container of sour cream
1 Bag Frozen Meatballs

Instructions

1) Empty the gravy into the Crock-Pot®, followed by the sour cream.

2) Combine these until they are completely blended.

3) Toss the package of frozen meatballs into the Pot filling to approximately 2/3 to ¾ of the space.

4) Place the lid on the pot and cook—occasionally stirring if you happen to be close to the kitchen.

5) You can always make more or less of the recipe depending on how many people you will serve.

Cooking Time: Low for a minimum of 5 hours

Sweet and Sour Chicken

Ingredients
1 (22-ounces) Bag frozen Tyson Chicken Breast
2 Cups cooked rice/steamed vegetables (or both)
1 bottle (18-ounces) Apricot Preserves
1 jar (12-ounces) chili sauce

Directions
1) Layer the frozen chicken pieces into the Crock-Pot®.

2) Combine the preserves and chili sauce in a small container (a mixing cup is ideal). Empty it over the chicken. *Note:* You can also use pineapple or a combination.

3) Toss to mix and let the Pot do the work.

4) Enjoy with some veggies and rice.

Servings: Six (one cup per serving)
Cooking Time on the high setting is 2 to 3 hours.

Creamy Taco Chicken

Ingredients

1 Can Rotel Original Tomatoes with Green Chilies
3 chicken breasts (no bone or skin)
4-ounces cream cheese (regular or light)
Directions

1) Pour the tomatoes, and place the chicken into the slow cooker.

2) A few minutes before the end of the cooking cycle, use a fork or

   tongs to shred the chicken.

3) Put the cream cheese on top of the mixture, but don't stir.

4) By the time the meal is ready, the cheese will be oozing into your

   chicken. Yummy!

Suggestions: You can use this in a casserole, over rice, as a salad, or any other creative plan you may have for your meal.
Cooking Time: Low temperature - Six to Eight hours

Stuffed – Roasted Turkey
Ingredients
2 C. Stuffing Mix
Black pepper and salt
6 Pounds Turkey
1 Tablespoon melted butter
Instructions

1) Use the package instructions to prepare the stuffing.

2) Flavor the turkey with some melted butter, pepper, and salt.

3) Prepare the bird by loosely placing the stuffing in the carcass.

4) Cover and let the Pot do the rest.

Servings: Four
Cooking Time: Low: 9 to 11 hours; High: 5 hours

Fish

Citrus Flavored Fish
Ingredients
Pepper and Salt
1 ½ pounds fish fillets
1 medium chopped onion
4 tsp. oil
5 Tbsp. Chopped parsley
2 tsp. Each grated: lemon and orange rind

Garnish: Lemon and orange slices
Directions
Use some butter to grease the Crock-Pot®.

1) Flavor the fish with some pepper and salt and put it into the pot.

2) Add the parsley, grated rinds, and onion as well as the oil over the

   fish.

3) Cover and cook.

4) When ready to eat; garnish with some lemon or orange slices.

Cooking Time: 1 ½ Hours on Low
Salmon Bake
Ingredients
3 (one-pound) Cans Salmon
1 (16-ounces) can tomato puree
4 cups bread crumbs (10 slices worth)
1 chopped green pepper
3 teaspoons lemon juice
2 crushed chicken bouillon cubes
1 Can each (condensed) cream of onion soup & cream of celery soup
6 (well-beaten) eggs
½ cup milk
Directions

1) Use some cooking spray or other oil to grease the Crock-Pot®

   lightly.

2) Blend all of the ingredients—except for the milk and celery soup

   into the Pot.

3) Cover and cook.

4) Combine and stir the milk and celery soup in a small pan to use

   as a sauce for the salmon.

5) When the salmon is done, garnish and enjoy with the special

   sauce!

Cooking Time: High for three hours or low for four to six hours

Pork

BBQ Style Pork Steaks
Ingredients
4 (½-inch cut) Pork shoulder steaks
2 large sliced tomatoes
1 large onion
1 large thinly sliced bell pepper
1 Tbsp. Each:

- Vegetable oil

- Tapioca (quick-cooking)

¼ C. red wine
½ tsp. cumin
½ C. barbecue sauce (your choice)
Directions
1) Slice and cut the onion as if you are preparing to make onion

   rings for dinner.

2) Trim away an excess fat and slice the steaks in half - lengthwise.

3) Brown the steaks in skillet using hot oil, and drain on paper

   towels.

4) Organize the peppers, tomatoes, and onions in the Crock-Pot®;

   sprinkling the tapioca over them. Place the pork in last.

5) Prepare the cumin, wine, and barbecue sauce in a small dish. Pour

   it over the ingredients in the Pot, and cover.

Servings: Four
Cooking Time: Low Heat – Six to Eight Hours (or until veggies and meat are tender)

Note: The recipe is based on a 3 ½- or a 4-quart Crock-Pot®. If you have a different size the cooking time may vary.

Pepsi® Roast

Ingredients

1 Can Cream of mushroom soup
5 Lb. Pork Roast/ Steak/Chops
½ package dry onion soup mix
1 can Regular Pepsi (Don't use Diet)

Directions

1) Put the meat in the Crock-Pot® first and sprinkle with the soup

   mix.

2) Empty the mushroom soup and Pepsi over the meat.

3) Close the lid and let the pot do the rest of the chore.

Suggestion: Use the sauce to pour over some rice or potatoes.
Servings: Eight
Cooking Time: Low setting for six to seven hours

Ranch Chops

Ingredients

Pouch – Ranch Dressing Mix
Pork Chops
1 Can Cream of Chicken Soup Plus (+) 1 Can Water OR 2 Cups Cream of Chicken

Directions

1) Pour the liquids into the Crock-Pot® along with the chops and

   dressing mix.

Cooking Time: Use the low-temperature setting for four to six hours.

Ham in Cider Gravy

This ham is so tasty it cannot remain in the 'breakfast only' slot. It is so tasty and can advance to lunch and dinner menus as well.

Ingredients

1 (one to four pound) Ham
¾ cup maple syrup
2 cups unsweetened apple cider
3 Tablespoons cornstarch

Directions

1) Arrange the ham in the Crock-Pot® and top it off with the syrup

   and cider.

2) Cook until the time indicated below is completed.

3) Move the ham to a serving platter. Pour the liquid into a large

   cup (a measuring cup is perfect).

4) Whisk ½ of the cider and the cornstarch on the stovetop using

   the low-temperature setting until it is smooth. Continue whisking

   and increase the burner to med-low—adding small amounts of

   cider at a time—until the gravy is bubbly and thickened to the

   desired consistency.

Servings: Four to Eight
Preparation Time: Four minutes
Cooking Time: Low - six to eight hours

Casseroles

Crock-Pot® Dinner: Beef or Chicken
Ingredients
1 Whole/cut up chicken –or- legs and thighs OR a Beef Roast
2 Carrots
4 Potatoes
5 Ounces water
1 Can celery or cream of mushroom soup (10 ¾ ounce)
Directions
1) Cut the carrots into four-inch chunks. Put all of the ingredients

   into the Crock-Pot®.

2) Set the Pot and let it 'go.'

Servings: Four
Cooking Time: The high setting will cook the meal in six hours, or you can cook it all day using the low-temperature setting.
Squash 'N Chops
Ingredients
5 Pork (boneless) Port cutlets or chops
2 medium oranges
1 ¼ Pounds delicate/butternut squash
1/8 tsp. Ground red pepper

½ tsp. Garlic salt
¼ tsp. Each: Ginger, cloves, and cinnamon
Directions

1) Peel and slice the oranges. Peel and slice the squash lengthwise and discard the seeds. Cut the 'half' into sections ½-inches thick.

2) Flavor the pork with some garlic salt and red peppers. Use a 4- to 5- quart Crock-Pot® and place the chops/cutlets in the bottom.

3) Combine the ginger, cinnamon, and cloves in a small dish.

4) Top off the pork with the oranges along with the toppings in step 3.

5) Cover and cook.

Servings: 5
Cooking Time: Low for 4 hours
Lasagna Enchantment
This one has a few more steps, but it is so worth it—and it's easy.
Ingredients
2 Cans diced tomatoes (28-ounces) drained
Four finely chopped clove of garlic
2 Tbsp. oregano
½ tsp. salt
15-ounces fresh ricotta
¼ tsp. pepper
½ tsp. salt
½ C. shredded Parmesan cheese
1 (12-ounce) Package uncooked lasagna noodles
½ tsp. fresh (finely chopped) parsley – more if desired
2 C. spinach leaves (bagged is okay)
2 C. shredded Mozzarella cheese
Directions

1) Mix the garlic, drained tomatoes, pepper, salt, and oregano in a mixing container.

2) In another bowl, blend the parsley, Parmesan, and ricotta cheese.

3) Dip anywhere from 1/3 to ½ cup of the tomato combination on

    the base of the Crock-Pot®.

4) Layer the noodles, spinach, several dollops of the ricotta combo,

    and 1/3 to about ½ of the tomato combination. Sprinkle the

    mozzarella on the top of that section. Continue the process with

    the mozzarella on the top.

5) Close the lid on the Pot and let it do the work.

Servings: Six to Eight
Prep Time: 20 Minutes
Cook Time: High is 2 Hrs. or Low is 3 to 4 Hrs.
Sweet Potato Casserole
Ingredients
1 ½ C. applesauce
1 tsp. ground cinnamon
3 Tbsp. Margarine/butter
½ C. Toasted chopped nuts
2/3 C. Brown sugar
6 medium sweet potatoes
Directions

1) Peel and slice the potatoes cutting them into ½-inch bits and

    drop them into a 3 ½-quart Crock-Pot®.

2) In a separate dish, mix the brown sugar, cinnamon, melted butter,

    and applesauce. *Note:* Be sure you pack the brown sugar tight

    when it is measured.

3) Empty the mixture over the potatoes in the Pot.

4) When the potatoes are tender; you can top with the chopped

    nuts. Yummy!

Cooking Time: Six to Eight hours

Sides/Veggies
Slow Cooked Baked Potatoes
Ingredients
6 Baking Potatoes
Kosher Salt
Oil
Garnishes: Your choice
Directions

1) Prepare the potatoes with a good scrub and rinsing, but do not

   dry them.

2) Put each one in some foil while poking holes in each one using a

   fork.

3) Use a small amount of oil to drizzle over each one adding a

   sprinkle of salt, and close the foil.

4) To keep them from getting soggy, ball up several wads of foil

   into the cooker.

5) Layer the potatoes on the balls and cover. Leave them on warm

   in the Crock-Pot® until ready to serve.

Cooking Time: Low – Six to Eight Hours
Corn on the Cob
Ingredients
3 ears or 5 to 6 halves – Corn on the cob
Salt as needed
1/2 stick or ¼ cup of softened butter
Directions

1) Shuck and remove the silks from the corn; break them into

   halves.

2) Cover each one with butter and wrap individually in foil.

3) Wad some foil balls up in the base of the unit and add about 1-inch of water.

4) Put the potatoes into the Crock-Pot®, and cook for the allotted time.

Servings: 4
Preparation Time: Five minutes
Cooking Time: Use the high setting for two hours. *Note*: The cooking time may vary if you prepare the corn with another unit besides a 5 to 6-quart pot.

Ranch Mushrooms

Ingredients
½ Cup Melted butter
1 Pound fresh mushrooms
1 Package - ranch salad dressing mix

Instructions

1) Leave the mushrooms whole and wash them well.

2) Put them into the Crock-Pot®, adding the oil and ranch mix by drizzling it over the mushrooms.

3) Cover the Pot. It is best to stir once after hour one to blend the butter.

Servings: Six
Cooking Time: Low will have your mushrooms ready in three to four hours.

Sweet Potatoes

Ingredients
4 medium sweet potatoes
Optional Garnishes:
Brown Sugar, Butter, Mini Marshmallows

Directions

1) Clean and prepare the potatoes—thoroughly dry.

2) Use a fork and poke holes in each one, and double wrap them in aluminum foil.

3) Put them in the Crock-Pot®--cooking them the specified amount

   of time. If you are close to the kitchen; turn and flip the potatoes

   in the pot occasionally.

4) Once they are done, add the garnishes of your choice and serve.

Servings: Four
Preparation Time: Five Minutes
Cooking Time: The Low setting is used for 8 hrs. or the High setting for 4 hrs. (Times may vary depending on the size of the potatoes, but you will know when they are ready by how soft the potato is when you give it a squeeze.)

Chapter 5: Desserts – Snacks & Treats to Devour

Apple Dump Cake

Ingredients

Butter (1 Stick)

Yellow cake mix (1 box)

Apple pie filling (1 Can)

Directions

1) Empty the apple filling into the Crock-Pot®.

2) *Dump* in the mix and then the butter on top of the mix.

Cooking Time: Cook the cake in the Pot on the low setting for approximately four hours for best results.

Enjoy!

Applesauce

Ingredients

12 Apples

1 teaspoon juice (+) ¼ of the lemon peel

2 cinnamon sticks

Directions

1) Peel, core, and slice the apples. Put the apples, lemon peel, and sticks into the Crock-Pot®.

2) Provide a drizzle to the top with the juice and set the cooking timer.

3) When the treat is ready—throw the lemon peel and cinnamon sticks into the garbage.

4) Blend with a regular or immersion blender.

5) Chill for a few hours.

Cooking Time is five to seven hrs.

Peach Cobbler

Ingredients

1 White cake mix (not prepared)

6 Large peaches

1- Stick (½- Cup) softened butter
Directions
1) Peel and slice the peaches, and put them into the Crock-Pot®.

2) Blend the butter and cake mix using a pastry blender. You want a

   crumbly texture.

3) Sprinkle the mix over the peaches, and cook.

Enjoy with a bowl of ice cream.
Servings: Eight
Preparation Time: Fifteen minutes
Cooking Times on the high setting is two to three hours; whereas the Low cycle will extend for about four hours.

Cocktail Franks – Sweet and Sour
Ingredients
40- Ounces Pineapple chunks
2 Pounds cocktail franks
1 Cup each:
- Grape jelly

- Chili sauce

3 Tablespoons each:
- Prepared mustard

- Lemon juice

Directions
1) Mix the jelly, chili sauce, mustard, and lemon juice in the Pot,

   mixing it well.

2) Cover and use the high setting for fifteen to twenty minutes to

   blend the ingredients

3) Slice the franks into bite-sized pieces and add to the Crock-Pot®.

4) Pour in the drained chunks of pineapple.

Servings: 10
Cooking Times: High setting for two hours; *Low* setting for four hours.

124

Index for the Recipes

Chapter 2: Healthy Breakfast Recipes

- Boiled Eggs

- One-Hour Bread

- Breakfast Fiesta Delight

- Italian Sausage Scramble

The Sweeter Side of Breakfast
- Blueberry Steel Cut Oats

- Pumpkin Pie Oatmeal

- Pumpkin Butter

Chapter 3: Time-Saving Lunch Specialties

- Beef Tacos

- Root Beer & BBQ Chicken

- Stuffed Banana Peppers

- Crock-Pot® Taco Soup

Chapter 4: Dinner in a Hurry
Beef
- Meat for the Tacos

- Steak Pizzaiola

- Steak in the Pot

Chicken & Turkey
- Buffalo Chicken

- Caesar Chicken

- Cranberry Chicken

- French Onion Chicken

- Hawaiian Chicken

- Honey Mustard Chicken

- Chicken Italian Style

- Swedish Meatballs

- Sweet and Sour Chicken

- Creamy Taco Chicken

- Stuffed – Roasted Turkey

Fish
- Citrus Flavored Fish

- Salmon Bake

Pork
- BBQ Style Pork Steaks

- Pepsi® Roast

- Ranch Chops

- Ham in Cider Gravy

Casseroles
- Crock-Pot® Dinner: Beef or Chicken

- Squash 'N Chops

- Lasagna Enchantment

- Sweet Potato Casserole

Sides & Veggies
- Slow Cooked Baked Potatoes

- Corn on the Cob

- Ranch Mushrooms

- Sweet Potatoes

Chapter 5: Desserts to Devour
- Apple Dump Cake

- Applesauce

- Peach Cobbler

- Cocktail Franks – Sweet and Sour

PART V

The following chapters will feature a wide variety of recipes that will fit anyone's tastes. There are simple recipes for the picky eater in your family and there are exciting recipes for that adventurous eater! Most of the ingredients are easy to find or ones that are already waiting in your freezer or pantry. Furthermore, most of these recipes are 'toss it in' types which means in the morning you toss in the ingredients and then go about your day. Then when you get home and eat your delectable meal, there are very few dishes to do! Anyone can learn to cook these recipes as there is little prep and no risk with open flames. Hopefully this book will open the meal possibilities and show the versatility of the Slow Cooker.

There are plenty of books on this subject on the market, thanks again for choosing this one! Every effort was made to ensure it is full of as much useful information as possible, please enjoy!

Chapter 1: Just For Starters

Do you have a party you want to bring a dish to? Maybe you just need a side dish to go along with a meal. Either way, the following recipes are great additions to any event or meal.

TACO DIP

5-7 hours in the slow cooker

Yields about 7 cups

14 ½ ounce can of tomatoes, stewed

15 ounce can of black beans, drained and washed

15 ¼ ounce can of corn, drained

1 taco seasoning envelope

8 ounce can of tomato sauce

16 ounce can of kidney beans, washed and drained

4 ounce can of green chilies, chopped

¾ cup(s) of chopped onion

Tortilla chips

Place everything into the slow cooker, excluding for the chips, then cook for 5-7 hours on low. Serve with Tortilla Chips.

MAC AND CHEESE

4 ½ hours in the slow cooker

Yields about 10 servings

16 ounce package of elbow macaroni

12 ounce can of evaporated milk

½ cup(s) of melted butter

1 cup(s) of milk

10 ¾ ounce can of cheddar cheese soup

2 beaten eggs

4 cup(s) of of cheddar cheese, shredded and divided

1/8 teaspoon(s) paprika

Make the noodles in accordance with the package directions and drain. Put pasta and butter into the slow cooker. Next, in a separate bowl mix the milk, soup, evaporated milk, eggs, and 3 cups of the cheese together. Pour the mixture in the cooker, stirring well. Cook for at least 4 hours on low. Lastly, add in what cheese and paprika is left and cook further until all is melted.

WILD RICE WITH MUSHROOMS

7-8 hours in the slow cooker

Yields about 12-15 servings

½ cup(s) of butter

1 cup(s) of brown rice

3-4 ounce cans of mushrooms

2 ¼ cup(s) of water

10 ½ ounce can of beef consommé

1 cup(s) of wild rice

10 ½ ounce can of French onion soup

Mix all ingredients in the cooker. Cook for 7-8 hours on the low setting.

CRAB DIP

3-4 hours in the slow cooker

Yields about 5 cups

1/3 cup(s) of salsa

½ cup(s) of milk

4 ounce can of chilies, chopped

3 packages of cubed cream cheese

1 cup(s) of of green onions, sliced thinly

2-8 ounce packages of real or imitation crab, flaked

Crackers

Coat slow cooker with nonstick spray and dump in milk and salsa. Mix until blended and add the remaining ingredients except for the crackers. Cook for 3-4 hours on low. Stir and serve on crackers.

PARTY BEANS

5-7 hours in the slow cooker

Yields about 14-16 servings

15 ½ ounce can of great northern beans, washed and drained

1/8 teaspoon(s) pepper

1 teaspoon(s) ground mustard

2 bay leaves

½ cup(s) of water

2-3 tablespoon(s) cider vinegar

½ cup(s) of brown sugar packed

1 chopped green pepper

1 chopped onion

1 chopped sweet red pepper

1 ½ cup(s) of ketchup

16 ounce can of kidney beans, washed and drained

15 ½ ounce can of black-eyed peas, washed and drained

15 ounce can of black beans, washed and drained

15 ounce can of lima beans, washed and drained

Combine everything into the slow cooker. Cooke for 5-7 hours on low.
Remove bay leaves and serve.

CHILI CHEESE SAUCE

45 minutes in the slow cooker

Yields about 20 servings

2-15 ounce cans of chili (no beans)

2 lb. brick of cheese, cubed

16 ounce jar of picante sauce

2-8 ounce packages of cream cheese

Mix everything into slow cooker. Cook for 45 minutes until everything is melted, mixed well, and warmed through. Serve with tortilla chips.

Chapter 2: Sandwiches That Will Melt in Your Mouth

These sandwiches or excellent for lunches, events and quick dinners! They will melt in your mouth and are sure to get you recipe requests.

BBQ CHICKEN SANDWICHES

6-8 hours in the slow cooker

Yields about 8-10 servings

6 cup(s) of of cooked, diced or shredded chicken

1 cup(s) of diced onion

1 ¼ cup(s) of ketchup

¼ cup(s) of brown sugar, packed

1 teaspoon(s) salt

¼ teaspoon(s) hot pepper sauce

¼ cup(s) of Worcestershire sauce

¼ cup(s) of cider vinegar or red wine vinegar

1 teaspoon(s) celery seed

2 cup(s) of water

1 teaspoon(s) chili powder

Buns

Merge all the components into the cooker except the buns and cook it for 6-8 hours on the low setting. Provide warm or toasted buns.

RANCH CHICKEN SANDWICHES

6-8 hours in the slow cooker

Yields about 6 servings

8 ounce of bacon bits

2 lbs. of chicken breasts, boneless

2 envelopes of dry Ranch seasoning

2-8 ounce blocks of cream cheese

Put the chicken, cheese and ranch into the cooker and it should cook for 6-8 hours on the low setting. Shred the chicken in the slow cooker with two forks, stir in the bacon bits and serve on warm or toasted buns.

HAM SANDWICHES

4-5 hours in the slow cooker

Yields about 12 servings

2 cup(s) of apple juice

½ sweet pickle relish

1 teaspoon(s) paprika

2 teaspoon(s) mustard

3 lbs. or about 40 slices of ham, sliced thin

Buns

2/3 cup(s) of brown sugar

Relish

Join the initial five ingredients in to a bowl. Layer the ham into the bottom of the slow cooker and then pour sauce on it. Cook for at least 4-5 hours on the low setting and serve on warm buns.

BEEF SANDWICHES

6-8 hours in the slow cooker

Yields about 8-10 servings

1 boneless chuck roast that is about 3-4 lbs.

¼ teaspoon(s) cayenne pepper

1 teaspoon(s) marjoram

1 teaspoon(s) caraway seeds

1 teaspoon(s) celery seed

2 teaspoon(s) garlic powder

2 teaspoon(s) oregano

2 teaspoon(s) salt

1 tablespoon(s) minced onion

1 teaspoon(s) rosemary

Buns

Mix all the seasonings and rub all over the entire roast. For 6-8 hours, cook on the low setting. Shred using two forks and serve on warm or toasted buns.

MEATBALL SUBS

6-8 hours in the slow cooker

Yields about 6 servings

1 cup(s) of milk

3 tablespoon(s) onion, chopped

¾ oats, quick-cooking

1 ½ teaspoon(s) salt

1 ½ lbs. ground beef

2 tablespoon(s) sugar

1 cup(s) of ketchup

3 tablespoon(s) vinegar

½ cup(s) of water

Buns

Provolone cheese

Break up meat into a bowl and combine with the first 4 ingredients. Roll meat into 1 inch balls and set all of them into a slow cooker. Grab a separate bowl and in it, combine, join the sugar, vinegar, ketchup, and water, then drizzle onto meatballs. For at least 6-8 hours, cook on the low setting and serve on toasted buns with or without cheese.

Chapter 3: Soups, Of Course!

No cookbook would be complete without some savory soups, especially a slow cooker book! Throw these together during a bitter winter day and warm up when you get home.

VEGETABLE SOUP

8 hours in the slow cooker

Yields about 8-10 servings

3 cup(s) of water

14 ½ ounce can of diced tomatoes, with liquid

1 lb. boneless round steak, cubed

2 potatoes, cubed

3 ribs of celery, sliced

1 large onion diced

2 carrots, sliced

½ cup(s) of corn

½ cup(s) of beans

½ cup(s) of peas

½ teaspoon(s) basil

¼ teaspoon(s) pepper

½ teaspoon(s) oregano

½ teaspoon(s) salt

3 cubes of beef bouillon

Mix everything into the slow cooker and then cook for about 8 hours on high.

TROUT CHOWDER

2 hours in the slow cooker

Yields about 6 servings

2 cup(s) of milk

1 cup(s) of cubed Monterey Jack cheese

¼ teaspoon(s) garlic powder

1 cup(s) of ranch salad dressing

10 ounce thawed package of frozen broccoli

1 lb. Trout filets with the skin removed (or some other white fish favorite)

1 tablespoon(s) butter

1 chopped medium onion

1 cup(s) of cubed cheddar cheese

Paprika

Place the first seven ingredients into the slow cooker and mix. Sauté the chopped onion in the butter and then toss it into the slow cooker. Next, cook for 2 hours on the high setting. When the dish is finished, the fish will flake very easily. Sprinkle each serving with some Paprika and serve with crackers or bread.

BUFFALO CHICKEN SOUP

4-5 hours in the slow cooker

Yields about 8 servings

3 cup(s) of cooked chicken

1/8 cup(s) of hot pepper sauce

6 cup(s) of milk

1 cup(s) of sour cream

3 10 ¾ ounce cans of cream of chicken soup

Join all the components into the cooker and for 4-5 hours, cook on the low setting.

WHITE CHILI

8-10 hours in the slow cooker

Yields about 12 servings

4 minced garlic cloves

2 chopped medium onions

1 teaspoon(s) salt

2 chicken bouillon cubes

½ teaspoon(s) ground cloves

2 teaspoon(s) oregano

2-4 ounce cans of green chilies

1 tablespoon(s) cumin

½-1 teaspoon(s) cayenne pepper

2 qt. of water

3 lbs. of boneless chicken without the skin

1 lb. dry navy beans

Shredded Monterey Jack cheese

Sour Cream

Chives, chopped

Put the garlic and onions into the cooker first and then put the remaining ingredients except the cheese, sour cream, and chives. For at least 8-10 hours, cook on the high setting. Stir and shred meat then serve with toppings of cheese, sour cream, and chives.

POTATO SOUP

7-8 hours in the slow cooker

Yields about 8-10 servings

5 cup(s) of water

¼ teaspoon(s) pepper

2 teaspoon(s) salt

¼ cup(s) of butter

4 teaspoon(s) chicken bouillon

½ celery, chopped

½ carrots, thinly sliced

2 cup(s) of onion, chopped

6 cup(s) of potatoes, cubed with or without skins

3 tablespoon(s) parsley

12 ounce can of evaporated milk

Chives, chopped

Place the first nine ingredients into the cooker and for at least 7-8 hours, cook on high. Include the parsley and milk, then stir. Continue cooking for an additional 30-60 minutes. Sprinkle chives on top.

Chapter 4: Juicy Beef

These recipes feature mouthwatering beef and common ingredients to make a meal everyone will love!

ITALIAN ROAST

8-9 hours in the slow cooker

Yields about 8-10 servings

½-1 teaspoon(s) salt

½ teaspoon(s) garlic powder

¼ teaspoon(s) pepper

1 boneless rump roast at around 3 ½ lbs.

1 diced medium onion

4 ½ ounce drained can of mushrooms

¼-1/2 cup(s) of beef broth or red wine

14 ounce jar of spaghetti sauce

Cooked Noodles

Merge the first 3 seasonings into a bowl and cut the roast in half. Rub the seasoning all over the roast and put it in the slow cooker. Top with the onions and mushrooms. Mix wine or broth with the spaghetti sauce and pour over everything in cooker. Cook for at least 8-9 hours on the low setting and serve.

CORNED BEEF AND CABBAGE

8-9 hours in the slow cooker

Yields about 6-8 servings

1 lb. baby carrots

4 potatoes, quartered with or without skin

1 medium onion, cut into large chunks

½ teaspoon(s) pepper

1 bay leaf

3 minced garlic cloves

2 tablespoon(s) cider vinegar

2 tablespoon(s) sugar

3 cup(s) of water

1 small head of cabbage sliced into chunks

1 corned beef brisket, about 3 pounds, with a spice packet

Put the first 3 ingredients into the cooker. Merge the water and spices into a separate bowl and pour into cooker. On top of the contents of the cooker, add your cabbage and brisket. Once all is in the cooker, cook for at least 8-9 hours on low. Remove bay leaf and serve.

SMOKEY BEEF AND BEANS

6-7 hours in the slow cooker

Yields about 8 servings

1 cup(s) of onion, chopped

1 lb. ground beef

¼ teaspoon(s) pepper

½ teaspoon(s) salt

1 teaspoon(s) liquid smoke

¼ cup(s) of brown sugar, packed

16 ounce can of drained and washed kidney beans

16 ounce can of drained butter beans

3 tablespoon(s) vinegar

2-16 ounce cans of beans and pork

1 cup(s) of ketchup

12 strips of cooked and crumbled bacon

Cook beef and onions until the beef is no longer pink in a skillet. Combine beef and onions and remaining components into the cooker and cook 6-7 hours on the low setting.

CHILI MAC

6 hours in the slow cooker

Yields about 12 servings

1 envelope chili seasoning

2 chopped green peppers

1 chopped onion

1 lb. ground beef

4 chopped celery ribs

8 ounce can of tomato sauce

2-15 ounce cans of hot chili beans with the liquid

7 ounce package of elbow macaroni

2 minced garlic cloves

Salt and Pepper

Mix the first 8 components into the cooker. For 6 hours, cook on low. Cook the noodles according to the package, drain and then stir into the chili. Serve warm with pepper and salt.

MUSHROOM BEEF OVER NOODLES

8 hours in the slow cooker

Yields about 6-8 servings

7.5 cans of French onion soup

7.5 cans of golden mushroom soup

¼ cup(s) of seasoned bread crumbs

10 ¾ cans of beefy mushroom soup

2 lbs. of beef stew meat, cubed

12 ounce package of wide egg noodles

Mix together the soups and bread crumbs right in the slow cooker, then add the beef. Cook for at least 8 hours on the low setting. Cook the noodles in accordance with the package directions and drain. Serve over noodles.

CASSEROLE THAT COOKS ITSELF

6-8 hours in the slow cooker

Yields about 12 servings

1 cup(s) of wild rice, rinsed

1 cup(s) of carrots, chopped

1 minced garlic clove

1 cup(s) of celery, chopped

2-4 ounce cans of drained mushrooms

1 chopped onion

3 beef bouillon cubes

½ cup(s) of slivered almonds

2 lbs. cubed boneless round steak

2 ½ teaspoon(s) season salt

3 cup(s) of water

Put ingredients into the slow cooker from the top of the list to the bottom, and do not stir. For 6-8 hours, cook on low. Stir and serve.

SPICY GOULASH

5-6 hours in the slow cooker

Yields about 12 servings

2-16 ounce jars of drained kidney beans

1 chopped onion

4-14 ¼ ounce cans of Mexican diced tomatoes with the liquid

2 cup(s) of water

1 lb. ground beef

2 tablespoon(s) chili powder

1 chopped green pepper

¼ cup(s) of red wine vinegar

1 tablespoon(s) Worcestershire sauce

1 teaspoon(s) basil

2 teaspoon(s) beef bouillon

1 teaspoon(s) parsley

¼ teaspoon(s) pepper

1 teaspoon(s) cumin

2 cup(s) of uncooked elbow macaroni

Cook beef in a pan until it is no longer pink. While it's cooking, place all other ingredients into the slow cooker, except noodles. Stir in cooked beef and cook for 5 hours on low. Stir in noodles for another 30 minutes and serve when the noodles are tender.

GOLOMBKI

6-8 hours in the slow cooker

Yields about 8 servings

1 lb. ground beef

1 cup(s) of converted rice, uncooked

1 small chopped onion

½ teaspoon(s) sugar

1 cup(s) of water

¾ teaspoon(s) salt

24 ounce jar of meatless spaghetti sauce

2-10 ¾ ounce tomato soup

¼ teaspoon(s) pepper

1 medium head of chopped cabbage

Cook onions and beef in a pan until no longer pink. Mix in salt, pepper, and rice. In separate bowl, combine sugar, water, spaghetti, and soup. In the slow cooker place 1/3 of the sauce mixture, ½ of the beef mixture and 1/3 of the cabbage. Repeat once, then dump in the rest of the sauce and remaining cabbage. For 6-8 hours, cook on low. Serve when rice is cooked.

SLOW COOKED MEAT LOAF

5-6 hours in the slow cooker

Yields about 6 servings

2/3 cup(s) of seasoned bread crumbs

½ teaspoon(s) rubbed sage

½ teaspoon(s) Worcestershire sauce

2 eggs

1 teaspoon(s) salt

¾ cup(s) of milk

2 teaspoon(s) minced onion

2 tablespoon(s) brown sugar

1½ lb. ground beef

¼ cup(s) of ketchup

1 teaspoon(s) ground mustard

Mix together the first 6 ingredients in a bowl, then stir in the ground beef well. Make into a loaf and for 5-6 hours, cook on low in the slow cooker.

In a different dish blend the remaining of the components and drizzle over the loaf. Cook for an additional 15 minutes and serve.

SLOW COOKER PIZZA

3 hours in the slow cooker
Yields about 6-8 servings

¼ cup(s) of chopped onion
4 ½ ounce can of drained mushrooms
26 ounce jar of spaghetti sauce
1 ½ teaspoon(s) Italian seasoning
3 cup(s) of shredded mozzarella cheese
16 ounce package of wide egg noodles
1 ½ lb. ground beef
3 ½ package of pepperoni
3 cup(s) of cheddar cheese, grated

Cook the onions and beef in a pan until no longer pink. At the same time, make the noodles in accordance with the directions on the package. Stir the Italian seasoning, mushrooms and spaghetti sauce in with the meat mixture. Drain noodles and set aside. In another separate bowl, mix the two cheeses together. In the slow cooker pour 1/3 of the meat mixture in the bottom, then 1/3 of the noodles, 1/3 of the pepperoni, and then 1/3 of the cheese. Repeat another two times. Cook for 3-4 hours on low until the cheese is melted.

Chapter 5: Tender Chicken

Everyone knows that chicken is the most versatile meat, but combine with a versatile appliance and you have never ending, time efficient and delicious meals!

CHICKEN IN A POT

7-9 hours in a slow cooker
Yields about 6 servings

2 celery ribs, chopped
2 medium onions, diced
½ teaspoon(s) pepper
3 medium carrots, sliced
1 ½ teaspoon(s) salt
3 medium carrots, sliced
1 teaspoon(s) basil
3 lbs. chicken
½ cup(s) of chicken broth

Layer the bottom of the cooker with the vegetables and top with the chicken parts. Mix the final components in a separate bowl and drizzle on top. Cook for 7-9 hours on low.

GOLDEN CHICKEN AND NOODLES

7-8 hours in the slow cooker

Yields about 6 servings

1/8 teaspoon(s) pepper

1 small chopped onion

2-10 ¾ ounce cans of broccoli cheese soup

1 teaspoon(s) basil

6 chicken breast cut in half

2 cup(s) of milk

1 teaspoon(s) salt

Cooked noodles

Mix together the first 6 ingredients. Place chicken parts in the cooker and top with the mixture. For 7-8 hours, cook on the low setting, until chicken juices run clear. Serve over noodles.

ORANGE CHICKEN

4-5 hours in the slow cooker

Yields about 4 servings

3 cup(s) of orange juice

1 cup(s) of green pepper, chopped

1 cup(s) of celery, chopped

3 lb. broiler chicken, cut into parts and skinless

4 ounce can of mushrooms

¼ teaspoon(s) pepper

½ teaspoon(s) salt

4 teaspoon(s) minced onion

1 teaspoon(s) parsley

3 tablespoon(s) cold water

3 tablespoon(s) cornstarch

Cooked Rice

Place the first 9 components into the slow cooker. Cook for at least 4 hours on the low setting. In a different bowl, mix the cornstarch with the water, and then stir into the sauce. After such, cook for another 30-45 minutes. Serve over hot rice.

CHICKEN DINNER

8-9 hours in the slow cooker

Yields about 4 servings

4 carrots, chopped into ½ inch pieces

1/8 teaspoon(s) garlic salt

10 ¾ ounce can of cream of chicken soup

6 red potatoes, chopped

4 chicken breasts

10 ¾ ounce can of cream of mushroom soup

2-4 tablespoon(s) of mashed potato flakes

Put carrots and potatoes into the of the slow cooker and then put in the chicken. In a different dish, mix the garlic salt and soups, then drizzle over the chicken. Cook for about 8-9 hours on low. If you want a thicker the gravy, you can add potato flakes and then cook for an additional 30 min.

CHICKEN A LA KING

8-9 hours in the slow cooker

Yields about 6 servings

3 tablespoon(s) flour

10 ¾ ounce can of cream of chicken soup

Dash of cayenne pepper

¼ teaspoon(s) pepper

½ cup(s) of green pepper, chopped

1 chopped celery rib

1 lb. of chicken breasts

¼ cup(s) of onion, chopped

10 ounce package of peas

2 tablespoon(s) pimentos, diced and drained

Hot cooked rice

Mix the first 4 ingredients into the slow cooker. Add the vegetables and chicken. Next, cook for 7 hours on the low setting and then add the pimentos and peas. Cook for at least 30 more minutes and serve over rice.

ITALIAN CHICKEN

4 hours in the slow cooker

Yields about 4 servings

1 envelope of dry Italian salad dressing

10 ¾ ounce can of cream of chicken soup

¼ cup(s) of water

8 ounce brick of cream cheese

4 ounce can of mushrooms, drained

4 chicken breasts

Hot cooked rice or pasta

Mix salad dressing and water in a small bowl. Put chicken in cooker and drizzle dressing over it. Cook for 3 hours on the low setting. Mix together the rest of the ingredients, except rice or noodles, and place in slow cooker. Stir mixture and continue cooking for an additional hour. Serve over rice or noodles.

APRICOT CHICKEN

4-5 hours in the slow cooker

Yields about 6 servings

2-12 ounce jars of Apricot preserves

6 chicken breasts

1 packet of dry onion soup mix

Hot cooked rice

Mix the soup mix and preserves. Drop chicken into the slow cooker and cover with preserves. Cook for at least 4-5 hours on the low setting and serve over rice.

CHICKEN CACCIATORE

6-8 hours in the slow cooker

Yields about 6 servings

2 onions sliced thin

1 bay leaf

2 minced garlic cloves

¼ teaspoon(s) pepper

8 ounce can of tomato sauce

½ teaspoon(s) basil

4 ounce can of mushrooms

1 teaspoon(s) salt

2 teaspoon(s) oregano

14 ½ ounce can of diced tomatoes

¼ cup(s) of water or dry white wine

3 lb. broiler chicken cut up into parts

Hot cooked pasta

Put the onions into the slow cooker. Top with the remaining components, except for pasta, then cook for about 6-8 hours on the low setting. Discard bay leaf and serve over pasta.

CHICKEN MOLE

6 hours in the slow cooker

Yields about 12 servings

1 teaspoon(s) salt

12 skinless chicken thighs

1 onion chopped

½ cup(s) of toasted sliced onions

2 dried ancho chilies, no stems or seeds

¼ cup(s) of raisins

3 tablespoon(s) olive oil

3 ounce chopped bittersweet chocolate

3 garlic cloves

28 ounce can of whole tomatoes, drained

1 chipotle pepper in adobo sauce

½ teaspoon(s) cinnamon

¾ teaspoon(s) cumin

Fresh cilantro

Put chicken into slow cooker and sprinkle with salt. Pu the rest of the components, except the cilantro, in a food processor and mix. Drizzle over chicken and cook for at least 6-8 hours on the low setting. Serve chicken with a pinch of cilantro.

CHICKEN MARINARA

4 hours in the slow cooker

Yields about 4 servings

1 minced garlic clove

1 chopped tomato

2 cup(s) of marinara sauce

1 ½ teaspoon(s) Italian seasoning

½ cup(s) of Italian salad dressing

4 chicken breasts

Hot cooked pasta

Shredded mozzarella cheese

Mix together the first 5 ingredients. Put chicken into slow cooker and cover with sauce. Cooke for 4 hours on low. Serve over pasta and sprinkle with cheese.

HONEY PINEAPPLE CHICKEN

3-4 hours in the slow cooker

Yields about 12 servings

8 ounce can of unsweetened crushed pineapple with the liquid

½ cup(s) of honey

2 tablespoon(s) soy sauce

1 cup(s) of brown sugar, packed

2 tablespoon(s) mustard

¼ cup(s) of melted butter

1/3 cup(s) of lemon juice

3 lbs. chicken breasts, skinless and boneless

2 tablespoon(s) canola oil

Brown chicken in a pan with the oil on both sides and place into the cooker. Next, mix together the last of the components and drizzle on chicken. Then, cook for 3-4 hours on low. Serve with pineapple chunks.

CHICKEN AFRITAD

7-8 hours in the slow cooker

Yields about 6 servings

½ cup(s) of soy sauce

½ cup(s) of olive oil

1 lb. chicken breasts, cubed

1 lemon juiced

Dash of pepper to taste

1 sliced green bell pepper

3 minced garlic cloves

1 cup(s) of green peas

1 sliced red bell pepper

3 cubed red potatoes

1 sliced yellow bell pepper

2 chopped carrots

1 sliced onion

2 cubed tomatoes

Put the first 5 ingredients into the slow cooker and let marinate for 10-15 minutes. Meanwhile mix the rest of the components together and pour into cooker after the chicken is done marinating. Cook for 7-8 hours on low.

Chapter 6: Flavorful Pork

Pork is one of those meats that is so flavorful. It can be paired with sweet fruits and preserves or mixed into a salty dish that is sure to please!

MUSHROOM PORK TENDERLOIN

4-5 hours in the slow cooker

Yields about 6 servings

10 ¾ ounce can of French onion soup

10 ¾ ounce can of golden mushroom soup

2-1 lb. pork tenderloins

10 ¾ ounce can of cream of mushroom soup

Mix together the soups in a bowl. Put tenderloin into the slow cooker then cover with soup. Cook for at least 4-5 hours on the low setting. Serve over rice or mashed potatoes.

SWEET AND SOUR RIBS

8-10 hours in the slow cooker

Yields about 8 servings

20 ounce can of pineapple tidbits, with liquid

½ cup(s) of of green pepper, thinly sliced

½ cup(s) of of onion, thinly sliced

¼ cup(s) of tomato paste

¼ cup(s) of cider vinegar

½ cup(s) of brown sugar, packed

2-8 ounce cans of tomato sauce

1 minced garlic clove

2 tablespoon(s) Worcestershire sauce

4 lbs. country style pork ribs, boneless

Salt and Pepper

Combine the top 9 ingredients into a bowl. Put ribs into the cooker then drizzle with the mixture. Cook for 8-10 hours on low. Thicken sauce if you desire and use salt and pepper to improve the taste if desired.

POLISH KRAUT AND APPLES

4-5 hours in the slow cooker

Yields about 4 servings

1 lb. of cooked Kielbasa or Polish sausage, chopped up

14 ounce jar of sauerkraut, drained and washed

3 medium tart apples, peeled then cut into wedges

¾ cup(s) of apple juice

½ teaspoon(s) caraway seed

1/8 teaspoon(s) pepper

½ cup(s) of brown sugar, packed

Put half of the sauerkraut into the slow cooker. Then put the apples and sausage and cap with remaining ingredient/sauerkraut. Cook for about 4-5 hours on low.

HAM AND HASH BROWNS

7-8 hours in the slow cooker

Yields about 4 servings

2 ounce jar of drained pimentos

2 cup(s) of of fully cooked ham, cubed

28 ounce bag of hash browns

10 ¾ ounce can of cheddar cheese soup

¼ teaspoon(s) pepper

¾ cup(s) of milk

Find a bowl and join the soup, pepper, and milk in it. Stir the pimentos, ham, and hash browns into the slow cooker. Mix in the soup and for 7-8 hours, cook on low then serve.

TENDER PORK ROAST

8-9 hours in the slow cooker

Yields about 8 servings

¾ cup(s) of soy sauce

8 ounce can of tomato sauce

½ cup(s) of sugar

2 teaspoon(s) ground mustard

3 lb. boneless pork roast

Get a bowl and combine the first 4 ingredients in it. Cut the roast in half and drop into the slow cooker. Top with the sauce and cook for about 8-9 hours on low.

PARMESAN PORK ROAST

5-6 hours in the slow cooker
Yields about 10 servings

½ teaspoon(s) salt
½ cup(s) of honey
2 tablespoon(s) olive oil
2 tablespoon(s) basil
2 tablespoon(s) minced garlic
3 tablespoon(s) soy sauce
4 lb. pork loin roast
2/3 cup(s) of grated parmesan cheese
2 tablespoon(s) cornstarch
¼ cup(s) of cold water

Get a bowl and combine the first seven ingredients in it. Afterwards, slice the pork in half and place in the cooker. Drizzle the sauce into the cooker and for at least 5-6 hours, cook on low. Remove roast and transfer liquid to a sauce pan. Mix the cornstarch with the water in a small bowl while bringing the pork sauce to a boil. Then stir in cornstarch and wait until it boils again and cook for another 2 minutes until it thickens. Slice roast and drizzle with gravy.

SLOW COOKER CHOPS

4-5 hours in the slow cooker
Yields about 10 servings

10 trimmed boneless pork chops
10 ¾ ounce can of cream of onion soup
1 large sliced onion
1 ounce packet of onion soup mix
1 ounce packet of ranch dressing mix
5 fluid ounce water

10 ¾ ounce can of cream of mushroom soup

Salt and Pepper

Put 1/3 of the onions in the slow cooker, then 5 of the chops. Repeat once more and then place remaining onions on top. Mix the rest of the components into a bowl and pour over the top. Cook for at least 4-5 hours on low and serve.

Chapter 7: Bonus! Desserts

What would life be without dessert? More importantly, what would a well-rounded cookbook be without the ability to help you make that dessert?

PUMPKIN PIE PUDDING

6-7 hours in the slow cooker

Yields about 6-7 servings

½ cup(s) of biscuit/baking mix

12 ounce can of evaporated milk

2 tablespoon(s) melted butter

15 ounce can of solid-pack pumpkin

2 beaten eggs

2 teaspoon(s) vanilla

2 ½ teaspoon(s) pumpkin pie spice

¾ cup(s) of sugar

Ice cream or whipped topping

Pour all the ingredients into a bowl, except the ice cream or whipped topping, and mix together. Spray the slow cooker with a nonstick spray and transfer pudding into cooker. Cook for 6-7 on low.

MINISTER'S DELIGHT

2-3 hours in the slow cooker
Yields about 10-12 servings

18 ¼ ounce box of cake mix
½ cup(s) of melted butter
21 ounce can of cherry or apple pie filling
1/3 cup(s) of chopped walnuts

In a bowl mix together butter and cake mix. Pour pie filling into slow cooker and cover with crumbly cake mix. Top with walnuts. Cook for 2-3 hours on low.

APPLE DELIGHT

3 hours in the slow cooker
Yields about 4-6 servings

¼ cup(s) of old fashioned oats
8 peeled and cored apples, sliced

¾ melted butter

2 tablespoon(s) lemon juice

¼ teaspoon(s) ground cinnamon

½ to 1 cup(s) of chopped pecans

1/3 cup(s) of sugar

Mix everything together in a slow cooker then for 3 hours, cook on the high setting. Stir occasionally.

CHOCOLATE PUDDING CAKE

6-7 hours in the slow cooker

Yields about 10-12 servings

3.9 box of chocolate pudding mix

¾ cup(s) of vegetable oil

4 eggs

1 cup(s) of water

2 cup(s) of sour cream

1 cup(s) of semisweet chocolate chips

18 ¼ ounce box of chocolate cake mix

Ice cream

Mix the top 6 components in a bowl for 2 minutes. Mix in the chocolate chips and coat slow cooker with a nonstick spray. Dump mixture into cooker and cook for between 6-7 hours on the low setting. Insert a toothpick into the middle of the cake; it's done when it comes out with moist crumbs. Serve warm with ice cream.

SWEET BREAD PUDDING

3 hours in the slow cooker
Yields about 6 servings

2 cup(s) of milk
¼ cup(s) of melted butter
¼ cup(s) of sugar
4 eggs
½ teaspoon(s) vanilla
¼ teaspoon(s) ground nutmeg
8 cup(s) of cubed old bread (white, wheat, Hawaiian, potato, cinnamon rolls, etc.)
1 cup(s) of raisins

Get a bowl and mix the first six ingredients in it. Put bread into the slow cooker and drizzle milk mixture on top. Top with raisins and cook for 3 hours on low.

SPICED APRICOT CIDER

2 hours in the slow cooker
Yields about 6 servings.

2-3-inch cinnamon sticks

2 whole cloves

2 cup(s) of water

¼ cup(s) of sugar

¼ cup(s) of lemon juice

2-12 ounce cans od apricot nectar

Combine all the components and for 2 hours, cook on low. Remove cloves and cinnamon sticks to serve. Replace a cinnamon stick into each cup(s) of if you want.

CPSIA information can be obtained
at www.ICGtesting.com
Printed in the USA
LVHW051957101220
673847LV00017B/2529